CAMBRIDGE LIBRARY COLLECTION

Books of enduring scholarly value

British and Irish History, Seventeenth and Eighteenth Centuries

The books in this series focus on the British Isles in the early modern period, as interpreted by eighteenth- and nineteenth-century historians, and show the shift to 'scientific' historiography. Several of them are devoted exclusively to the history of Ireland, while others cover topics including economic history, foreign and colonial policy, agriculture and the industrial revolution. There are also works in political thought and social theory, which address subjects such as human rights, the role of women, and criminal justice.

Memoir of John Aubrey

The antiquarian and topographer John Britton (1771–1857) is best remembered for his multi-volume series of *The Beauties of England and Wales*. A self-taught author and scholar, he was attracted by the work of John Aubrey (1626–97), who was born in the same Wiltshire village as him, and had very similar interests as an antiquarian and biographer, famous for his *Brief Lives* and for his surveys of and writings on Avebury and Stonehenge. Britton's research on Aubrey's life induced him to write a fresh account, using surviving manuscripts as well as printed sources, which would clear up the contradictions and errors of earlier versions. This 1845 book is a fascinating portrait of a sickly child who ended up a pauper because of family debts and lawsuits, but was a diligent and intelligent scholar, scientist and occultist, and a close friend of Thomas Hobbes and Robert Hooke.

Cambridge University Press has long been a pioneer in the reissuing of out-of-print titles from its own backlist, producing digital reprints of books that are still sought after by scholars and students but could not be reprinted economically using traditional technology. The Cambridge Library Collection extends this activity to a wider range of books which are still of importance to researchers and professionals, either for the source material they contain, or as landmarks in the history of their academic discipline.

Drawing from the world-renowned collections in the Cambridge University Library and other partner libraries, and guided by the advice of experts in each subject area, Cambridge University Press is using state-of-the-art scanning machines in its own Printing House to capture the content of each book selected for inclusion. The files are processed to give a consistently clear, crisp image, and the books finished to the high quality standard for which the Press is recognised around the world. The latest print-on-demand technology ensures that the books will remain available indefinitely, and that orders for single or multiple copies can quickly be supplied.

The Cambridge Library Collection brings back to life books of enduring scholarly value (including out-of-copyright works originally issued by other publishers) across a wide range of disciplines in the humanities and social sciences and in science and technology.

Memoir of John Aubrey

Embracing his Auto-Biographical Sketches,
a Brief Review of his Personal and Literary Merits,
and an Account of his Works

JOHN BRITTON

CAMBRIDGE
UNIVERSITY PRESS

CAMBRIDGE
UNIVERSITY PRESS

University Printing House, Cambridge, CB2 8BS, United Kingdom

Cambridge University Press is part of the University of Cambridge.
It furthers the University's mission by disseminating knowledge in the pursuit of
education, learning and research at the highest international levels of excellence.

www.cambridge.org
Information on this title: www.cambridge.org/9781108073448

© in this compilation Cambridge University Press 2014

This edition first published 1845
This digitally printed version 2014

ISBN 978-1-108-07344-8 Paperback

Engraved by C.E.Wagstaff, from a Drawing by Faithorne in the Ashmolean Museum.

JOHN AUBREY.

(Born A.D. 162⅚ — Died 1697)

Proof

For Britton's Memoir of Aubrey — Wiltshire Topographical Society.

MEMOIR

OF

JOHN AUBREY, F.R.S.

EMBRACING HIS

AUTO-BIOGRAPHICAL SKETCHES,

A BRIEF REVIEW OF HIS PERSONAL AND LITERARY MERITS,

AND AN ACCOUNT OF HIS WORKS;

WITH

Extracts from his Correspondence,

ANECDOTES OF SOME OF HIS CONTEMPORARIES,

AND OF THE TIMES IN WHICH HE LIVED.

BY

JOHN BRITTON, F.S.A., &c.

Lower Easton-Pierse, Wiltshire, the birth-place of John Aubrey.

Published by the Wiltshire Topographical Society.

LONDON:
PRINTED BY J. B. NICHOLS AND SON, 25, PARLIAMENT STREET.

1845.

TO THE MOST NOBLE,

HENRY, MARQUESS OF LANSDOWNE,

&c. &c. &c.

AS PATRON OF THE WILTSHIRE TOPOGRAPHICAL SOCIETY;

AS RESIDING IN THE VICINITY OF THE NATAL HOME OF JOHN AUBREY, AND OF THE
AUTHOR OF THE PRESENT MEMOIR;

AS A LOVER OF GENERAL LITERATURE AND THE FINE ARTS;

AND AS A STATESMAN WHO HAS EVER ACTED WITH CONSISTENCY AND DEVOTED ATTENTION
TO THE WELFARE AND HONOUR OF HIS COUNTRY,

THIS VOLUME IS INSCRIBED,

WITH SENTIMENTS OF SINCERE RESPECT AND ADMIRATION,

BY THE AUTHOR.

March, 1845.

PREFACE.

ANXIOUSLY desiring to see the *Wiltshire Topographical Society* in active and useful operation, I regret that my intended, and long promised, *History and Description of the Parish of Kington St. Michael* has been from time to time delayed, by illness, and such pressing avocations, as have hitherto prevented my proceeding with it.

I have always contemplated, as a portion of that work, a biographical notice of JOHN AUBREY, who was a native of the parish; considering such notice to be an essential feature of the publication. No topographical work can be deemed complete without authentic accounts of those persons who, by their acts and deeds, their genius and talents, or any other qualities, whether of good or evil, have conferred importance or notoriety upon the locality referred to, either as the place of their birth or temporary abode: and this principle is sanctioned by the authority and practice of all modern topographers and county historians. A place may confer an honorary title and some distinction on a person who has no other claims to popularity; but the talents and fame of the man generally stamp importance and interest on his birth-place. Stratford is noted for its Shakspeare, Lichfield for Garrick and Johnson, Woolsthorpe for Newton, and Knoyle for Wren.

In examining the published accounts of John Aubrey's literary and personal career, I soon found that several of the circumstances and dates mentioned in them were inconsistent, contradictory, and improbable, and appeared to rest on slight foundations;—that the information to be gathered from them was very unsatisfactory and imperfect; and that an attentive perusal even of his printed works, would supply better details of his life and actions. I had long possessed some extracts of a personal nature from his manuscripts in the Ashmolean Museum, Oxford, and was persuaded that a careful examination, not only of those papers—of which, in fact, no *complete* list has hitherto been printed—but of his writings in other places, was essential to the preparation of a correct and judicious biography.

Although at the risk of extending this Memoir to a length which might be deemed disproportionate to its importance, I resolved to undertake such examination and scrutiny: and have consequently reconciled many apparent contradictions, and corrected many errors, in former memoirs; besides meeting with some additional circumstances of great value, as illustrating not merely Aubrey's life and writings, but the state of society in general, and especially the literary opinions and tone, of the seventeenth century.

It is true I have not been able to present a minute chronological narrative, such as Evelyn, Pepys, Ashmole, Wood, Dugdale, Thoresby, and some others, have afforded by their journals or memorandum-books. Each of those distinguished persons bequeathed to posterity valuable and interesting Diaries and Autobiographies, referring to their various public works and private habits, as well as to their "sayings and doings;" whence we are enabled to understand and appreciate their peculiar characteristics, almost as if we had been personally familiar with them. The celebrated Dr. Stukeley,—who was a zealous and indefatigable collector and recorder of opinions and events,—left a similarly minute account of all that he saw and learned, during his long intercourse with antiquaries, historians, and other men of letters and science. These memoranda, occupying several quarto and octavo volumes, together with a series of letters addressed to the Doctor by eminent persons, and a collection of his miscellaneous writings, have been many years in my possession: and they would have been given to the world, had I been insured against the risk of loss from their publication. Aubrey himself appears to have kept a Diary; but neither this nor many others of his *private* papers, have been preserved; and, except as to the events mentioned in his auto-biographical memoranda, I have been compelled to glean the facts here laid before the public, from his correspondence, and from incidental passages and occasional reminiscences in various parts of his works.

By the course thus adopted, I have produced at least a consistent and authentic memoir; and if it tends to increase the reputation of John Aubrey as a zealous and industrious antiquary, and an honourable and upright man, I shall be rewarded for the labour it has involved.

Himself a judicious and discriminating biographer, it is remarkable that Aubrey should have been so slightly noticed by those who have professed to write accounts of his life and literary works. A short notice of these will shew what has been the result of their labours. *Some Account of this Work and its Author*, was prefixed by Dr. Richard Rawlinson, of St. John's College, Oxford, to Aubrey's *History of Surrey*, which the learned Doctor published, with additions by himself, in the year 1719. This was the earliest memoir of Aubrey; and it was founded in part on information given to Dr. Rawlinson " by a very worthy gentleman, a native of Wiltshire," who derived his materials " from Mr. Aubrey's own writing, as well as from some printed authorities." Dr. Rawlinson also alludes to "a reverend divine from Kington St. Michael's," as giving him other information. The memoir, however, is extremely incorrect in many parts. The next account was called, *Some Memoirs of the Life of Mr. John Aubrey*, and was published in his *Miscellanies,* 2nd edition, 1721. The author of the article *Aubrey*, in the *Biographia Britannica* (1747), conjectures that it was by the same writer as the previous memoir. It is shorter, but in many parts a mere transcript of Dr. Rawlinson's paper; and although in one passage an error in the first notice is corrected, in another place a date, before correctly given, is perverted. The article in the *Biographia Britannica* was probably written by Dr. Kippis, and is certainly compiled with care and discrimination. It corrects some of the most palpable errors of Dr. Rawlinson, and points out their origin : but, whilst it affords a favourable view of the literary merits of our antiquary, it adds little or nothing to the previous accounts of his personal character. Thomas Warton, in his *Life of Bathurst* (8vo.

1761), speaks highly of Aubrey's industry and learning, and had evidently examined some of his manuscripts at Oxford, but he merely mentions him incidentally. Jointly with William Huddesford, of Trinity College, Oxford, Warton edited the *Lives of Leland, Hearne, and Wood* (2 vols. 8vo. 1772); and in a note to the auto-biography of the last writer they directed public attention to Aubrey's papers, by giving an imperfect list of them. The works of Granger, Chalmers, and indeed all the principal Biographical Dictionaries and Encyclopædias, since Aubrey's time, foreign as well as English, contain notices of him : but, passing over most of these, and merely remarking that the memoir in Malcolm's *Lives of Topographers* (4to. 1815), is the most inaccurate and careless of any that have been written, I may advert with very different feelings to the articles in the *Penny Cyclopædia*, in Rose's *Biographical Dictionary*, and in the *Biographical Dictionary published by the Society for the Diffusion of Useful Knowledge :* the first, written by G. L. Craik ; the second, by the Rev. Joseph Hunter, ; and the third, by J. T. Stanesby. These manifest an earnest desire for precise and literal accuracy ; and, though in each some of the errors of the former Lives are retained, they are undoubtedly the best accounts of Aubrey hitherto published. Mr. Stanesby's article calls for especial commendation ; and it is only to be regretted that the nature of the work of which it forms a part, forbade that minute research and exposition which, with greater latitude of time and space, would have enabled the writer to have formed an interesting and complete memoir.

I may here observe, as a singular feature in the previous biographies of Aubrey, that the date of his birth has been erroneously stated in some of them; and that, until now, neither the day nor even the year of his death, nor the place of his interment, has been correctly ascertained. After a series of inquiries in many quarters, as to his death and burial, resulting only in disappointment, it was at last almost by accident, that I was directed, by a manuscript note of Dr. Rawlinson's, to the church of St. Mary Magdalene, at Oxford; on searching the registers of which, Dr. Ingram found the record of his burial. It is surprising that a man so well known to the literati of Oxford should quit the scene of life thus unregarded by his contemporaries and immediate successors, and that nearly a century and a half should have elapsed before the publication of this obituary record.

That the present memoir has been the result of extensive and diligent research and inquiry must be apparent to every reader: that it is not more copious and complete, no one can regret more than myself; for the subject and the times to which it refers are replete with interest, as well as with important matter for the consideration of the biographer and historian: and materials for their further elucidation once existed, and perhaps are still concealed in some obscure, unexplored repository. I have devoted many years to inquiry and collection, and sought for information from every available source. In some instances, indeed, I have to apprehend that such inquiries have been deemed impertinent, or too troublesome to be noticed; as I have written letters to two principal descendants of the Aubrey family without obtaining replies. I have been likewise unsuccessful in procuring any account either of the present owner of the *Monumenta Britannica* (mentioned in page 87), or of its condition. On the death of Mr. Churchill, of Henbury, the Dorsetshire parts of his library and property were sold by auction, and it is not unlikely that the manuscript referred to was amongst the objects then disposed of. Some of the unsold books descended to his cousin the late Sir Charles Greville, and from that Baronet were transferred to his brother, the present Earl of Warwick, who, in answer to my application, very promptly and politely writes, that he cannot find any trace of the Aubrey manuscript in his collection.* It is lamentable and surprising that four volumes of such writings should thus be so heedlessly neglected, and perhaps lost.

However indifferent and apathetic the great bulk of the nobility, gentry, and clergy of the county of Wilts may be to the literature which is devoted to its history and antiquities, or to the Society which is now formed to promote inquiry on those topics, and to publish the results; the time will soon arrive, when a better and more enlightened policy and practice must arise; for the effects of literature and mental improvement on the human race seem to be almost commensurate with those of steam on commerce, trade, and the social condition of man. Ignorance

---

* I have also been aided in my fruitless search after this manuscript by the Rev. W. Churchill, of Colliton, Dorsetshire, by S. H. Gummer, Esq. of Bridport, J. S. Wickens, Esq. and Samuel Forster, Esq. of London.

will not only be regarded as disreputable, but as a moral vice: and a knowledge of local history as an essential qualification to every person who aspires to a respectable station in society.

The labour and research bestowed upon the present volume fully exemplify the remarks of the learned and experienced Bacon:—" Out of monuments, names, words, proverbs, traditions, private records and evidences, fragments of stories, passages of books, and the like, we do save and recover somewhat from the deluge of time."—*On the Advancement of Learning, Book ii.*

In closing this explanatory notice, it is a pleasing duty to express my thanks to P. B. DUNCAN, Esq. the Keeper, and to Mr. KIRTLAND, the Deputy Keeper, of the Ashmolean Museum, for the courtesy with which they permitted ready access to, and extracts to be made from, Aubrey's papers in that collection. Although the account which I have given of those papers is more copious than originally intended, I cannot suppose it will in any way supersede or interfere with the catalogue of them which I understand is preparing by W. H. BLACK, Esq.

Although the fees for searching and examining the archives of that valuable Museum are comparatively moderate, I think they should not be required from professional authors; for, added to travelling expenses, residence from home, &c. such charges tend to make authorship expensive.

I owe some valuable suggestions and improvements in this work to my friend the Rev. Dr. INGRAM, the President of Aubrey's College (Trinity), at Oxford, to JOHN GOUGH NICHOLS, Esq. F.S.A., and to PETER CUNNINGHAM, Esq.

To Mr. T. E. JONES I am obliged for much useful aid, in searching for and collecting materials, from various public libraries, and from a vast mass of miscellaneous books and papers.

CONTENTS.

ILLUSTRATIONS.

MEMOIR OF JOHN AUBREY, F.R.S.

Chap. I.

AUTO-BIOGRAPHY—INTRODUCTORY NOTICE OF AUBREY'S LITERARY WORKS, CORRESPONDENTS, AND
FRIENDS—HIS LOVE OF ANTIQUITIES—A BIOGRAPHER AND TOPOGRAPHER—HIS HISTORY OF
SURREY, AND COLLECTIONS FOR WILTSHIRE—HIS CREDULITY AND SUPERSTITION—HIS AUTO-
BIOGRAPHICAL NOTES—LIST OF HIS WORKS.

THE AUTO-BIOGRAPHY of a person who has attained deserved distinction, if written with honesty and judgment, is among the most useful and interesting of literary productions. If " the proper study of mankind be man," that study can never be better or more profitably pursued than in the unprejudiced and unvarnished confessions of one, who, having investigated his own moral and mental attributes, and those of his associates, has learned to " know himself." Courage to acknowledge his own weaknesses and errors, constitutes an essential item in the wisdom of man. As the portrait of a great artist, by himself, is estimable and valuable, so is the auto-biography of any person who has rendered service to his species. Such portraits as those of Titian, Rembrandt, Rubens, and Reynolds, by each of those accomplished artists, make pleasurable and indelible impressions on the eye and memory; and such auto-biographies as those of Benvenuto Cellini, of Gibbon, of Hume, of Gifford, and of Franklin, not only furnish valuable materials for the philosopher, but are replete with interest and excitement,—with precept and example,—with entertainment and instruction, to the general reader.

If the following memoir be less attractive than either of those above referred to, it will still afford some pleasing glimpses of an interesting period in the literary history of England; and it will be found to place in a favourable light the character of one whose merits as an antiquary and as a man have not been hitherto sufficiently acknowledged. The name of JOHN AUBREY, though familiar to most antiquaries and biographers, and duly appreciated by them, is perhaps unknown to many readers

B

of the present volume. Portions of his literary works have, it is true, been published;* but one of them was on a subject long since trodden down by the "march of intellect;" another has been superseded by more recent and superior publications on the same theme; and the rest, having only had a limited circulation, hold but a subordinate place in the annals of fame.

To excite the curiosity of the general reader, and to point out the interest which must attach to a narrative of Aubrey's career, it may be necessary to premise that he was contemporary, and on intimate terms, with a great number of men illustrious in science, philosophy, literature, and art.

To enumerate indeed the whole of his correspondents and familiar friends would be to give a list of all the distinguished persons whose learning graced the latter half of the seventeenth century: some of them, however, may be mentioned in proof of this assertion. Connected himself with the Royal Society even before its incorporation, and appointed a Fellow under the charter which was granted by King Charles the Second, he was acquainted with its first President, Lord Brouncker, and still more intimate with those ornaments and professors of practical science which that Society fostered and encouraged; Newton, Halley, Flamsteed, Hooke, Wallis, Holder, Sir

* The following are their title-pages. I. "MISCELLANIES: viz. I. Day Fatality. II. Local Fatality. III. Ostenta. IV. Omens. V. Dreams. VI. Apparitions. VII. Voices. VIII. Impulses. IX. Knockings. X. Blows Invisible. XI. Prophecies. XII. Marvels. XIII. Magic. XIV. Transportation in the Air. XV. Visions in a Beril or Speculum. XVI. Converse with Angels and Spirits. XVII. Corpse Candles in Wales. XVIII. Oracles. XIX. Ecstasies. XX. Glances of Love and Envy. XXI. Second-sighted Persons. Collected by J. AUBREY, Esq. London. Printed for Edward Castle, next Scotland-Yard-Gate, by Whitehall, 1696." 12mo. Reprinted, with additions and alterations, in 1721 and 1784.

II. "THE NATURAL HISTORY AND ANTIQUITIES OF THE COUNTY OF SURREY. Begun in the year 1673 by JOHN AUBREY, Esq. F.R.S., and continued to the present time. Illustrated with proper sculptures. London. Printed for E. Curll, in Fleet-street, 1719." 5 vols. 8vo.

III. "LETTERS WRITTEN BY EMINENT PERSONS IN THE SEVENTEENTH AND EIGHTEENTH CENTURIES: to which are added, Hearne's Journeys to Reading, and to Whaddon Hall, the Seat of Browne Willis, Esq. and LIVES OF EMINENT MEN, by JOHN AUBREY, Esq. The whole now first published from the originals in the Bodleian Library and Ashmolean Museum, with biographical and literary illustrations; in two volumes. London. Printed for Longman and Co. 1813." 8vo.

IV. "AN ESSAY TOWARDS THE DESCRIPTION OF THE NORTH DIVISION OF WILTSHIRE. By me JOHN AUBREY, of Easton Pierse. Typis Medio-Montanis, Impressit C. Gilmour, 1838." 4to. Printed for Sir Thomas Phillipps, Bart.

V. "ANECDOTES AND TRADITIONS. Edited by W. J. Thoms. Printed for the Camden Society, 1839," 4to. The second part of this volume contains sixty-nine short extracts from AUBREY'S MANUSCRIPT "REMAINS OF GENTILISME," in the British Museum, with explanatory and illustrative notes by the Editor.

William Petty, Evelyn, Sir Christopher Wren, Gale, Harvey, Ray, and many others. Thomas Hobbes, and Sir James Harrington, William Penn, and Isaac Walton, honoured him with their friendship, which was duly appreciated by him in return. The poets Butler, Cowley, Denham, Waller, D'Avenant, and Dryden; the antiquaries Dugdale, Wood, Gibson, Tanner, Plot, and Llhwyd; the artists Hollar, Cooper, Faithorne, and Loggan, all held frequent intercourse with Aubrey, who was besides esteemed and patronized by several of the prelates, judges, and enlightened nobles of the age. His unpublished memoranda and correspondence contain varied and interesting materials for further illustration of the characters and writings of many of those celebrated men.

The principal feature in John Aubrey's literary character was his love of antiquarian pursuits. He may be regarded as essentially an *Archæologist*, and the first person in this country who fairly deserved the name. Historians, chroniclers, and topographers there had been before his time; but he was the first who devoted his studies and abilities to archæology, in its various ramifications of architecture, genealogy, palæography, numismatics, heraldry, &c. No one before him investigated or understood anything of the vast Celtic temple at Avebury, and other monuments of the same class; and certainly no person had preceded him in attempting to distinguish the successive changes, in style and decoration, of ancient ecclesiastical edifices, or to ascertain, by observing architectural features and details, to what era any particular building belonged. Aubrey's remarks on this subject are certainly interesting, and their publication at the present day, when the study of architectural antiquities is so deservedly general and popular, would add much to his credit as a careful and discriminating observer and delineator of the peculiarities of Christian architecture.* The present memoir will necessarily be too brief even for a short analysis of them.

It is hardly too much to say that modern antiquaries owe their knowledge of the great Celtic temple, at Avebury, in Wiltshire, entirely to Aubrey. Had he not first

* These papers descended from Mr. Awnsham Churchill, a celebrated bookseller of Aubrey's time, to the late Wm. Churchill, Esq. of Henbury, in Dorsetshire, at whose death they appear to have been sold by auction. They are a part of Aubrey's manuscript *Monumenta Britannica*, abridgements of which are in the Bodleian Library; at Stourhead, Wilts; and in my own collection.

called attention to that wonderful work, it may be doubted whether Dr. Stukeley
would afterwards have examined and described it; and so many years might thus
have elapsed that successive mutilations would have rendered it impossible for more
recent writers to trace its original arrangement and extent. Aubrey too was the
first whose published opinion pronounced this monument, with Stonehenge and
similar stone circles, to be religious temples raised by the British Druids; an opinion
which has since been more generally entertained by antiquaries than any of the
speculations before promulgated upon the subject. On this point, as in most of his
theories, regarding either the works of nature or of art, Aubrey's views were generally
useful, practical, and rational, and in these respects afford a striking contrast to
the visionary ideas of his learned and vigilant successor, Dr. Stukeley.

To those who are already familiar with the name of Aubrey he is known as a
biographer and a topographer. In the former department his collections are
unquestionably valuable. It is impossible to read his biographical notices without
appreciating the industrious and pains-taking accuracy of his information, and at the
same time admiring the vivacious and animated manner in which the most minute
circumstances are narrated. With few and trifling exceptions, the sources from
which Aubrey gained his information stamp these notices with a character of
authenticity. It is not, perhaps, generally known how much, in these matters,
Anthony à Wood's valuable *Athenæ* and *Fasti Oxonienses* are indebted to his labours.

Aubrey's *History of Surrey*, published by Dr. R. Rawlinson, with additions
by himself, was by no means equal to the elaborate topographical works of
Dugdale. Still it was an acceptable contribution to that class of literature; and
its accuracy in matters of detail is highly commended by Manning and Bray,
whose labours in the same field qualified them to form an opinion on the subject.
Aubrey's collections in illustration of the natural history, topography, and antiquities
of *Wiltshire*, his native county, are not only copious and valuable in themselves, but
highly interesting as the earliest extant. They were evidently executed *con amore*, and
with a competent knowledge of the subjects treated of; which, as will be hereafter
shown, were not confined to architectural and genealogical details. One portion of
these collections has been published by Sir Thomas Phillipps, Bart. (Vide p. 2.)

Though Aubrey appears to have resided chiefly in London, he was frequently in Wiltshire and at Oxford, and travelled into South Wales, Surrey, Herefordshire, and other parts of England, and once visited the continent. With a naturally curious and inquiring mind, he lost no opportunity in these excursions of obtaining traditionary and personal information. So early as the days of Hearne this peculiarity had procured for him the character of a "foolish gossip;" indeed Ray, the distinguished naturalist, in one of his letters to Aubrey, cautions him against a too easy credulity. Influenced by a querulous passage in Anthony à Wood's Diary, some recent writers have regarded him as a mere idle tale-bearer; but it is hoped that the present memoir will correct this erroneous impression. The following are passages in Ray's letter to Aubrey, and in Hearne's works, respecting him :

"I think," says Ray, "(if you can give me leave to be free with you,) that you are a little inclinable to credit strange relations. I have found men that are not skilfull in the history of nature very credulous, and apt to impose upon themselves and others, and therefore dare not give a firm assent to anything they report upon their own authority, but are ever suspicious that they may either be deceived them_ selves, or delight to teratologize, (pardon ye word,) and to make shew of knowing strange things."*

Hearne, in his *MS. Collections for the year* 1710,† says, "Mr. Aubrey gave Anthony à Wood abundance of informations; and Anthony used to say of him, when he was at the same time in company, 'Look, yonder goes such a one, who can tell such and such stories; and I'le warrant Mr. Aubrey will break his neck down stairs rather than miss him.'" The same writer thus mentions him more fully in his *Account of some Antiquities in and about Oxford:* ‡ "Before the destruction made in the late *horrid rebellion* (against King Charles the First,) the tower of the church [of Oseney Abbey, near Oxford] and divers other parts were standing, as may be seen in the second volume of the *Monasticon Anglicanum* (page 136), where they are delineated by the care and at the charge of the late Mr. John Aubrey, who

* Original, Ray to Aubrey; dated Black Notley, 8^{br}. 27, (16)91, in vol. ii. of a collection of *Letters to Aubrey*, in the *Ashmolean Museum.*

† Vol. xxvi. p. 39 (as quoted by Dr. Bliss in his edition of Wood's *Athenæ Oxonienses*, i. clxix).

‡ Printed at the end of vol. ii. of *Leland's Itinerary.*

began the study of antiquities very early, when he was gentleman-commoner of Trinity College in Oxford, and had no inconsiderable skill in them, as may appear from his history of the Antiquities of Wiltshire, his native county, now remaining in the Museum Ashmoleanum; which work, though imperfect and unfinished, yet evidently shows that he could write well enough upon a subject to the study of which he was led by a natural inclination; and the world might have justly expected other curious and useful notices of things from him, both with respect to the antiquities of Oxford, as well as those in his own and other countries, had not he, by his intimate acquaintance with Mr. Ashmole, in his latter years too much indulged his fancy, and wholly addicted himself to the whimseys and conceits of astrologers, soothsayers, and such like ignorant and superstitious writers, which have no foundation in nature, philosophy, or reason. But notwithstanding this unhappy avocation, which brought innumerable inconveniences along with it, he was otherwise a very ingenious man, and the world is indebted to him for so carefully preserving the remains of this old Abbey of Osney, and for assisting Mr. Wood and others in their searches after antiquities, and furnishing them with several excellent memoirs concerning this as well as other monasteries of this kingdom."

When Malone was preparing his *Life of Shakespeare,* he had recourse to Aubrey's manuscripts at Oxford, and in a paper which he intended as an *appendix* to that memoir* he has given a good summary of Aubrey's literary character. In one passage he observes, " However fantastical Aubrey may have been on the subjects of chemistry and ghosts, his character for veracity has never been impeached, and as a very diligent antiquarian his testimony is worthy of attention. Mr. Toland, who was well acquainted with him, and certainly a better judge of men than Wood, gives this character of him: 'Though he was extremely superstitious, or seemed to be so, yet he was a very honest man, and most accurate in his accounts of matters of fact. But the facts he knew, not the reflections he made, were what I wanted.' [*Toland's Specimen of a Critical History of the Celtick Religion,* p. 122."]†

---

* It is printed at p. 694 of the second volume of Boswell's edition of Shakespeare (8vo, 21 vols., 1821).

† The entire passage from Toland's work deserves to be quoted. " John Aubrey, Esq. a member of the Royal Society, (with whom I became acquainted at Oxford, when I was a sojourner there,) was the only

Malone adds, "I do not wish to maintain that all his accounts of our English writers are on these grounds to be implicitly adopted; but it seems to me much more reasonable to question such parts of them as appear objectionable, than to reject them altogether because he may sometimes have been mistaken." Malone refers to Aubrey's account of Shakspere as that of "an ingenious man, and a most careful, laborious, and zealous collector of anecdotes relative to our English poets, and other celebrated writers." Even in refuting the statements both of Rowe and Aubrey, as to the supposed occupation of the poet's father, he says, "I do not think it necessary or becoming to throw any ridicule on either of these gentlemen, nor shall I represent them as foolish gossips, because they have transmitted to us such accounts on this subject as they could procure. And I shall particularly abstain from ridiculing Mr. Aubrey (whose name ought never to be mentioned by any friend to English literature without respect), on account of the tradition he has transmitted," because, as he proceeds to show, it arose from a mistake into which Aubrey might easily have been led.*

This is valuable and discriminating testimony; and contrasts strongly with the hasty notices by D'Israeli, who, with less than his usual sagacity and penetration, characterizes Aubrey as "too curious and talkative an inquirer," and likewise as "the little Boswell of his day."†

In addition to these opinions, the following remarks, hitherto unpublished, are added from the pen of the Rev. Dr. Ingram, whose studies and attainments confer authority and value on his testimony: "Aubrey's Life of the great mathematician,

person I ever then met who had a right notion of the temples of the Druids, or indeed any notion that the circles so often mention'd were such temples at all, wherein he was intirely confirm'd, by the authorities which I show'd him, as he supply'd me in return with numerous instances of such monuments, which he was at great pains to observe and set down. And tho' he was extremely superstitious, or seem'd to be so: yet he was a very honest man, and most accurate in his accounts of matters of fact. But the facts he knew, not the reflections he made, were what I wanted. . . . . Sir Robert Sibbald, in his *History of Fife,* affirms, that there are several Druids' temples to be seen everywhere in Scotland, particularly in the county he describes. 'These (says he) are great stones plac'd in a circle, at some distance from each other,' &c. Mr. Aubrey show'd me several of Dr. Garden's letters from that kingdom to the same purpose, but in whose hands now I know not." *Toland s History of the Druids,* edited by R. Huddleston. 8vo. 1814, p. 159.

* *Life of Shakespeare, by Malone,* in *Boswell's edition,* vol. ii. p. 73.

† *Quarrels of Authors,* vol. iii. pp. 55, 76.

Oughtred, proves how much the world is indebted to him; but envy, malice, and sciolism, must have their day. He was too laborious a man to be properly appreciated in an age of superficial acquirements and controversial excitement, two evils which generally combine to retard and obstruct intellectual vigour. I could say much on this head, but I forbear, lest, as Selden says, 'some conscious man may take it as a libel.'"

Aubrey's biographers have all in succession expatiated on his deluded attachment to the study of judicial astrology, on his belief in ghosts, and other supernaturals, as calculated to detract from his just merits as an antiquary and topographer. That he was deeply imbued with superstition, and a credulous believer in all the absurdities of the so-called *science* of astrology, is sufficiently proved by his *Miscellanies*, unfortunately the only work he published during his life. But it should be borne in mind that this was a failing incidental to the age in which he lived, and especially to the circle in which he moved; and that the same aberration of good sense prevailed in the poet Dryden, the statesman Clarendon, the monarch Charles I., and many other eminent and illustrious men. In fact, although persons of Aubrey's station in society, in the present age of intellectual advancement, no longer entertain the same prejudices and fallacies, this improvement is of more recent date than is perhaps generally supposed, and certainly far less extensively diffused than could be desired. Within my own recollection, most of the inhabitants of Aubrey's native parish were sincere and ardent believers in the appearance of ghosts, in haunted houses, in witchcraft, in necromancy, in fairies, and their manufactory of grass rings, in the supernatural influence of jack-a-lanterns, or will-o'-the-wisps, and many other visionary vagaries, which belonged not merely to the lower and middle, but to the educated and higher classes of society.

Even in our own age an implicit belief in the mysteries of astrology is hardly exploded. The annual predictions of " Francis Moore, physician," in his *Vox Stellarum*, still mystify and seduce their hundreds, nay thousands, of readers; and the experiment, once tried, of excluding them from his almanac proved so unsuccessful, that its proprietors (though unwilling to impose on the credulity of the public) have found it inexpedient to risk the popularity of so profitable a work by again attempting it. Meantime "Oracles of Fate," "Prophetic Messengers," and similar works, emanating from authors with the sounding names of "Raphael," "Zadkiel," &c. frequently issue from the press ; and even in the present year (1845) a weekly paper, price one penny, to be called "The Astrologer," is announced to appear in London. This is described as "the most wonderful publication of the day," and "the most startling and entertaining work ever issued." It is asserted that "the student in astral science will here find ample directions for acquiring a knowledge of this truly wondrous and prophetic art." "Astrology," it further says, "is now avowedly studied in both the Universities, and a society (the Rosicrucian Association) openly exists, and holds its meetings for the advancement of the science in the Metropolis." In this truly "*startling work*," "predictions of the weather and to events from week to week will be given as a proof of the *sublime truths* on which the study is based !"

From circumstances like these it is clear that a belief in supernatural appearances and influences is not, and perhaps never will be, wholly eradicated from the human mind, and that there still remains much to be done in the way of general education check its progress, to expose its absurdities, and to inculcate maxims of sound and genuine philosophy.

Sir Walter Scott, in his *Letters on Demonology and Witchcraft*, characterizes the astrology of Aubrey's time as "the queen of mystic sciences, who flattered those who confided in her, that the planets and stars, in their spheres, figure forth and influence the fate of the creatures of mortality, and that a sage acquainted with her lore could predict, with some approach to certainty, the events of any man's career, his chance of success in life or in marriage, his advance in favour of the great, or answer any other *horary questions*, as they were termed, which he might be anxious to propound, provided always he could supply the exact moment of his birth. This, in the sixteenth and greater part of the seventeenth centuries, was all that was necessary to enable the astrologer to erect a scheme of the position of the heavenly bodies, which should disclose the life of the interrogator, or Native, as he was called, with all its changes, past, present, and to come. Imagination was dazzled by a prospect so splendid ; and we find that in the sixteenth century the cultivation of this fantastic science was the serious object of men whose understandings and acquirements admit of no question . . . . . The earlier astrologers, though denying the use of all necromancy, that is, unlawful or black magic, pretended always to a correspondence with the various spirits of the elements, on the principles of the Rosicrucian philosophy. They affirmed they could bind to their service, and imprison in a ring, a mirror, or a stone, some fairy, sylph, or salamander, and compel it to appear when called, and render answers to such questions as the viewer should propose." Of this class of visionaries, who, though of later date than the alchemists, sometimes combined the pursuit of alchemy with astrology, the famous Dr. Dee may be regarded as the type. "A grave and sober use of this science," Sir Walter Scott continues, "would not have suited the temper of those who, inflamed by hopes of temporal aggrandizement, pretended to understand and explain to others the language of the stars. . . . . Such being the case, the science was little pursued by those who, faithful in their remarks and reports, must soon have discovered its delusive vanity through the splendour of its professions; and the place of such calm and disinterested pursuers of truth was occupied by a set of men, sometimes ingenious, always forward and assuming, whose knowledge was imposition, whose responses were, like the oracles of yore, grounded on the desire of deceit, and who, if sometimes they were elevated into rank and fortune, were more frequently found classed with rogues and vagabonds." These remarks he proceeds to illustrate by reference to William Lilly's *History of his Life and Times*,* from which it is evident that Lilly was extremely cunning, ignorant, coarse, and vulgar, but well fitted to dupe the silly and more ignorant persons who applied to him for advice. He was born in 1602, began to study astrology in his thirtieth year, and died in 1681. It has been often charitably supposed that Lilly was himself a believer in the prophetic powers of which he boasts himself possessed, and this has arisen from the simplicity and apparent candour of his narrative; but there is quite enough in his remarkable work to stamp

---

* Scott has further exposed the meanness and chicanery of the alchemists and astrologers in his admirable novels, *Kenilworth* and *Quentin Durward*. The reader who may be desirous of pursuing this subject further will find it ably illustrated in a series of papers in the *Penny Magazine* (1843), and in the article *Astrology*, in the *Penny Cyclopædia*: works which have been greatly beneficial in ministering to that desire of knowledge which now characterizes all classes of readers.

him as a crafty person, if not a knave and an impostor. The accounts this book contains of Dr. Dee, Kelly, Forman, Evans, and other artful pretenders to astrological knowledge, and its illustrations of the public events, and the general customs of his time, certainly render it one of much curiosty and interest. Lilly, says Sir Walter Scott, "maintained some credit even among the *better classes*, for *Aubrey* and *Ashmole* both called themselves his friends, being persons extremely credulous, doubtless, respecting the mystic arts." Hearne, as we have seen, attributes Aubrey's partiality for these pursuits to his intercourse with Ashmole; but his works in general show that he was even less superstitious than the latter, who in his turn was far superior to Lilly. Ashmole's *Diary* exhibits the same, or even greater, coarseness and vulgarity of language than Lilly's *History*, whilst it is also full of triviality of detail: but he had greater advantages of education and wealth than Lilly, and his works on Berkshire, and the Order of the Garter, together with the noble Museum founded by him at Oxford, entitle him to the lasting gratitude of posterity. He was born in 1617, and died in 1692. Wharton, Coley, Gadbury, and others, were celebrated at the period alluded to amongst the professors of astrology. Of the class at large Scott says, "There was no province of fraud in which they did not practise: they were scandalous as panders; and, as quacks, sold potions for the most unworthy purposes."

The downfall of astrology was effected by a combination of causes. The great discoveries in astronomy, soon after the formation of the Royal Society, proved the fallacy of the views on which the "celestial scheme," or "horoscope,"* was drawn. The degraded character of its professors naturally led to the degradation of the art itself; and perhaps the quaint, satirical, *Hudibras* of Butler had some share in producing this result. The three parts of that celebrated poem were published from 1663 to 1678, and the character of *Sidrophel* affords a strongly marked and ludicrous picture of the judicial astrologer of the time. It is probable that this character was intended as a satire upon Lilly, who is at all events expressly ridiculed in the same work, under the names of "English Merlin"† and "Erra Pater." The

---

* This was a diagram showing the supposed positions of certain of the heavenly bodies at the time to which it referred. See p. 13.

† Lilly published an almanac for many years successively with the title of "*Merlinus Anglicus, junior*, English Merlin revived." He is satirised by Congreve in "Love for Love."

opcration of these causes became manifest very soon after Aubrey's death; and it is
not too much to infer that, had he lived a few years more, his treatise on " Hermetick Philosophy," as he terms the *Miscellanies*, would never have been published.
His sagacity and shrewdness on other subjects justify the belief that, in a more
enlightened age, he would have been amongst the first to discountenance and expose
the fallacies of that " occult science."

The leading features in Aubrey's literary and mental character, thus generally
noticed, are further exemplified in the following *Auto-biographical* notices of his
early life and studies, copied from the manuscript of his *Lives of Eminent Men*,
in the Ashmolean Museum, Oxford. These reminiscences were probably overlooked
when the selection from those lives was published, in the work entitled *Letters from
the Bodleian Library ;*—for, holding his literary labours, as the editors* of that
publication did, in such high esteem, it is not otherwise easy to account for their
omission. These notes, which are now printed for the first time, were evidently
written (as were the majority of the memoirs in the same work) at different times;
the facts being narrated in a loose and vague manner, and blanks left for names,
dates, and sums, which, not occurring to Aubrey's recollection when he wrote, were
never afterwards supplied. They are covered with interlineations and marginal
additions, and in many parts so illegibly written that it is difficult to decipher many
of the words. The singular and unaccountable transitions from the first to the third
person in the manuscript, from which the following is printed, are remarkable.
The article is here given verbatim : the heading prefixed to it shows how little
value Aubrey set upon it himself.

I. A.

To be interponed † as a sheet of wast paper only at the binding of a booke.

This person's life is more remarqueable in an Astrologicall respect, then for any advancement of learning,
having, from his birth (till of late yeares) been labouring under a crowd of ill directions :‡ for his escapes of

---

* The Rev. Dr. Bliss, and the late Rev. J. Walker, of New College, Oxford.

† INTERPONED; from the Lat. *inter* and *pono*, to set or insert between. [*Webster.*]

‡ An astrological expression, meaning, under the influence of evil planets.

many dangers in journeys both by land and water. He was borne at Easton Pierse, (a hamlet in the parish of Kington Saint Michael,) in the hundred of Malmesbury,* in the countie of Wilts, (his Mother's inheritance, D. and H. of Mr. Isaac Lyte), March the 12, (St. Gregories day,) A.D. 1625, about sun-riseing ; being very weak, and like to dye, that he was christned before morning prayer.

I gott not strength till I was 11 or 12 yeares old, but had belly ake, paine in the side, sicknesse of vomiting for 12 houres, every fortnight for . . . yeares, then about monethly, then quarterly, and at last once in half a yeare : about 12 it ceased.

When a boy bred at Eston, (in Eremiticall solitude,) was very curious, his greatest delight to be with the Artificers that came there, e. g. joyners, carpenters, cowpers, masons, and understood their trades ; horis vacuis, I drew and painted. In 1634 was entred in his Latin gramer by Mr. R. Latimer, a delicate and little person, rector of Leigh-de-la-mere, — a mile, fine walk,—who had an easie way of teaching ; and every time we asked leave to go forth, we had a Latin word from him, wch at our returne we were to tell him again : which in a little while amounted to a good number of words.

HOROSCOPE OF JOHN AUBREY'S NATIVITY, from his own sketch.

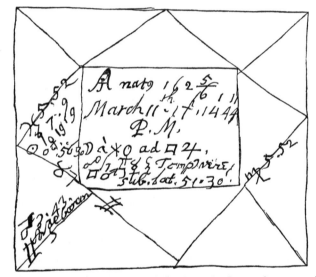

'Twas my unhappinesse in half a year to lose this good enformer by his death, and afterwards was under severall dull ignorant teachers till 12, 1638, about which time I was sent to Blandford schoole, in Dorset. W. Sutton, B.D. who was ill natured. Here I recovered my health, and got my Latin and Greeke. Our usher had (by chance) a Cowper's Dictionary, which I had never seen before. I was then in Terence. Perceiving his method, I read all in the booke where Ter. was, and then Cicero, which was the way meanes by which I got my Latin. 'Twas a wonderfull helpe to my phansie in reading of Ovid's Metamorph. in English by Sandys, which made me understand the Latin the better. Also I mett accidentally a book of my Mother's,— Bacon's Essayes,—which first opened my understanding on the moralls, (for Tullies Offices were too crabbed for my young yeares,) and the excellent clearnesse of the style, and hints, and transitions.

I was alway enquiring of my grandfather of the old time, the rood loft, &c., ceremonies of the Priory, &c. At 8 I was a kind of Engineer, and I fell then to Drawing, beginning first with plaine outlines, e. g. in

---

* Aubrey errs in placing Easton in the hundred of Malmesbury, as it belongs to that of North Damerham.

draughts of . . . . .; then on to colours, being only my owne instructor. Copied pictures in the parlor in a table book. I was wont (I remember) much to lament with myselfe that I lived not in a city, *e. g.* Bristole where I might have access to watchmakers, locksmiths, &c. Not very much care for gram̄. Apprehensive enough, but my memorie not tenacious, so that then a boy, I was a promising morne enough, of an inventive and philosophicall head. My witt was alwaies working, but not to verse. Exceeding mild of spirit, mightily susceptible of fascination. Strong and early impulse to antiquities. Tacitus and Juvenal. Look't through logique and some ethiques.

He began to enter into pocket mdm books, philosophicall and antiquarian remarques A°. D. 1654, at Llantrithid.

1642, May 2. I went to Oxford. Peace. But now did Bellona thunder, and as a cleare skie is sometimes suddenly overstretched with a dismall black cloud and thunder, so was the serene peace by the civill war, through the factions of those times. In August following my father sent for me home for feare. In Febr. following (with much importunity) I gott my father to lett me go to beloved Oxford againe (then a garrison pro Rege). I got Mr. Hesketh, a priest, Mr. Dobson's man, to drawe the ruines of Osney 2 or 3 wayes before 'twas pulled downe ; now the very foundation is digged up. In April I fell sick of the small pox at Trin. Coll ; and when I recovered, after Trin. weeke, my father sent for me into the country again, where I conversed with none but servants and rustiques, (to my great greefe, for in those days fathers were not acquainted with their children,) and soldiers quartered. Odi prophanum vulgus et arceo. It was a most sad life to me then, in the prime of my youth, not to have the benefitt of an ingeniouse conversation, and scarce any good bookes. Almost a consumption. This sad life I did lead in the country till 1646, at which time I got (with much adoe) leave of my father to let me goe to the M. Temple. April 16, 1646, admitted. 24 June following Oxon was surrendered, and there came to London many of the King's party, with whom I grew acquainted (many of them I knew before). I loved not debauches, but their martiall conversation : was not so fit for the messe. Novemb. 6 I returned to Trin. Coll. in Oxon. again to my great joy : was much made of by the fellows, had their learned conversation, lookt on books, musique. Here and at M. T. (off and on) I (for the most part) enjoyed the greatest felicity of my life. [Ingeniouse youths, like rose buds, imbibe the morning dew.] Till Dec. 1648 (Xmas eve,) I was sent for home from Oxon again to my sick father, who never recovered, where I was engaged to look after his country business, and solicite a lawe suite. A° 165-, Octob. —, my father dyed, leaving me debts 1800 lib., and law proceed. 1000 lib. A° 16— I began my lawe suite on the entaile in Brecon, which lasted till . . . . . , and it cost me 1200 lib. A° . . . I was to have married Mrs. K. Ryvs, who dyed when to be married. . . . . 2000 lib., besides counting one of her brothers 1000 lib. p. ann.

A° . . . I made my will, and settled my estate on trustees, intending to have seen the antiq. of Rome and Italy, and then to have returned and married ; but (Diis aliter visum est superis) viz. . . . . . to my inexpressible griefe and ruine, hindered the designe, which was my . . . . cause. But notwithstanding all these embarrassments, I did . . . . (as they occurred) tooke notes of antiq., and having a quick draught, have drawn landskips on horseback symbolically, *e. g.* journey to Ireland in July, A° Dom. 166-.

The debts and lawe suites . . . . borrowing of money, and perpetuall riding to my . , . . Aº . . . . sold manor of Burleton, in Heref. to Dr. F. Willis. Aº . . . sold the manor of Strafford * to Herbert, Lᵈ Bp. of Hereford. Aº 1664, June 11, went into France. Octob. . . . . returned. Then Joan Sumner . . . , then lawe suite wᵗʰ her, then sold Easton Pierse and the farme at Broad Chalke. Lost 500ˡⁱ . . +200ˡⁱ. goods and timber. Absconded as a banished man. Ubi in monte Dei videbitur. I was in as much affliction as a mortall could bee, and never quiet till all was gone. Submitted my selfe to God's will; wholly cast my selfe on God's providence. I wished Monasterys had not been put downe, that the Reformers would have been more moderate as to that point. . . . . fitt there should be receptacles and . . . . for contemplative men . . . . this compensated; wᵗ a pleasure 'twould have been to have travelled from monastery to monastery. The Reformers in the Lutheran countries were more prudent then to destroy them, *e. g.* in Halsatia, &c. Nay, the Turks have monasteries; why should our Reformers be so severe ?

Never quiett, nor anything of happiness till ᵈⁱᵛᵉˢᵗᵉᵈ ᵒᶠ ᵃˡˡ, all was sold, 1670, 1671. at what time Providence raysed me, (unexpectedly, good friends), the Right Hon. Nicholas E. of Th., † with whom I was delitescent ‡ . . . . at Hethfield, in Kent, neer a year, and then was invited . . . . Then Edm. Wyld, Esq. R.S.S. of Glazely Hall, Salop, tooke me into his armes, with whom I most commonly take my diet and sweet otiums.

Aº 1671 having sold all and disappointed as aforesaid of moneys I recᵈ, I had so strong an impulse to (in good part) finish the Description of Wilts, in 2 volumes in fol., that I could not be quiett till I had donne it, and that with danger enough, tanquam canis e Nilo, for feare of crocodiles (*i.*) catchpoles. And indeed all that I have donne, and that little I have studied, has been just after that fashion; so that, had I not lived long, my want of leisure would have afforded but a slender harvest of . . . . . A strange fate that I have laboured under, never in my life to enjoy one entire moneth, (*i.* once at Chalke, in my absconding, Aº . . .) or 6 weeks otium for contemplation. My studies in geometry were on horseback and the house of office : so I gott my algebra : Oughtred in my pocket, with a little information from Edw. Davenant, D.D. of Gillington, Dorset. My father discouraged me. My head was alwaies working, never idle, and even travelling (which from 1649 till 1670 was never off my horse back,) did gleane some observations, of which I have a collection in folio of two quire of paper, some whereof are to be valued.

My fancy lay most to geometrie. If ever I had been good for anything 'twould have been a painter. I could fancy a thing so strongly, and have so cleare an idea of it.

Stomach so tender that I could not drinke claret without sugar, nor white wine but 'twould disgorge; not well recovered till 1670.

---

* This word is illegibly written. It probably means Stretford, near Leominster, Herefordshire.

† Nicholas Tufton, 3rd Earl of Thanet. He was twice imprisoned in the Tower by Cromwell on suspicion of conspiracy against the Protector and his council, and died 24th Nov. 1679.

‡ DELITESCENCE, (*delitescentia*, Lat.) retirement, obscurity. [*Johnson.*]

When a boy he did ever love to converse with old men as Living Histories : he cared not for play, but on play dayes he gave himselfe to drawing and painting.   Never riotous or prodigall, but (as Sir E. Leech s^d) sloath and negligence, carlessnesse, =valent [equivalent] to all other vices.
_{lachese}

Whereas very sickly in youth, Deo gratias, healthy from 16 . .

AMICI.

A. Ettrick, Tr. Coll.	A. Wood, 1665.
Fr. Potter, of C.C.C.	Bp. Sarum.
M. T. Jo. Lydall.	Dr. W. Holder.
Sir J. Hoskyns, Baronet.	Sir William Petty, my singular friend.
Ed. Wyld, Esq. of Glazely Hall.	Sir James Long, Baronet, of Draycot.
Mr. Rob. Hooke, Gresh. Coll.	Mr. Ch. Seymour, . . of the D. of S.*
Mr. Hobbes, 165-.	

I now indulge my genius wth my friends, and pray for ye young angells rest, at Mrs. Mores, neer Gresh. Coll.

I. A. lived most at Broad Chalk, in Com. Wilts.   Sometimes at Easton Piers.   At London every terme. Much of his time spent in journying to S. Wales,—Entaile,—and Heref.sh.

SCRIPSIT, Naturall History of Wiltshire.
>   Idea of Education of the Noblesse from the age of 10 or 11 till 18.   In Mr. Ashmole's hands.
>   Item, Remaynders of Gentilisme, being Observations of Ovid's Fastorum.
>   Mem.   Villare Anglicanum interpreted.
>   Item, Faber Fortunæ.   For his owne private use.
>   These lives p. A. W.† 16⅞⅞.

It was I. A. that did putt Mr. Hobbes upon writing his Treatise de Legibus, which is bound up with his Rhetorique ; that one cannot find it but by chance.   No mention of it in the first title.

Mem. I. Aubrey, in the year 1666, wayting then upon Joan Sumner, to her brother at Seen, in Wilts, there made a discovery of a chalybiate waters, and these more impregnated than any waters yet heard of in England.   I sent some bottles to the R. S. in June, 1667, which were tryed with galles before a great assembly there.   It turns so black that you may write legibly with it, and did there, after so long a carriage, turn as deepe as a deep claret.   The physitians were wonderfully surprised at it, and spake to me to recom-

---

* [Brother of Francis, 5th Duke of Somerset, on whose death, in 1678, he succeeded to the title.]
† [These Lives for Anthony à Wood.]

mend it to the D^{rs} of the Bath, (from whence it is but about 10 miles,) for that, in some cases, 'tis best to begin with such waters and end with the Bath, and in some *vice versa*. I wrote several times, but to no purpose, for at last I found that, though they were satisfied of the excellency of the waters, and what the London D^{rs} sayd was true, they did not care to have company goe from the Bath. So I inserted it the last yeare in M. Lilly's alm. and towards the latter end of summer there came so much company that the village could not containe them, and they are now preparing for building of houses against the next summer. Jo. Sumner sayth (whose well is the best,) that it will be worth to him 200 lib. p^r ann. Dr. Grew, in his History of the Repository of the R. Society, mentions this discovery, as also of the iron oare there, not taken notice of before. 'Tis in part III. c. ii. pag. 331.*

Another auto-biographical paper by Aubrey was in the possession of Dr. Rawlinson, who quoted it in the memoir prefixed to the History of Surrey. That paper is not amongst the doctor's manuscripts in the Bodleian Library, but a copy of it, by Mr. Ballard, is appended to a volume of his valuable and interesting series of *Original Letters,* preserved in that collection ; and, as apposite to the subject of the present memoir, it is added in the ensuing page. It may be observed that the title of this paper, " *Accidents* of John Aubrey," does not necessarily denote *misfortunes,* though few of the circumstances mentioned were of any other kind ; the word *accidents* is an astrological term, and means simply *events* or *occurrences,* such as were supposed to have been influenced by the position of the heavenly bodies at the time of a person's birth.

* Aubrey appears to have thought very highly of these discoveries, and used every exertion to make them available for useful purposes. Amongst others he succeeded in interesting Sir James Long, of Draycot, in the subject. The " Seen water" is frequently mentioned in his papers ; and in his *Natural History of Wiltshire, Chap.* ii. on *Springs Medicinall,* is a more minute account of it than the above. He there states that he made the discovery " at the Revell there, 1665. Whereupon I sent my servant to the Davises for some galles to try the waters, and made my first experiment at Mr. Jo. Sumner's (where I lay)." " This advertisement," he says, " I desired Dr. Rich. Blackburne to word. He is one of the College of Physitians, and practiseth yearly at Tunbridge Wells. It was printed in an almanack of Hen. Coley about 1681, but it tooke no effect. It was about 1688 before they became to be frequented." — " Advertisement. At Seen (near the Devises, in Wiltshire), are springs, discovered to be of the nature and virtue of those at Tanbridge, and altogether as good. They are approved of by severall of the physitians of the colledge in London, and have donne great cures, viz. particularly in the spleen, the reines, and bladder, affected with heat, stone, or gravell, or restoring hectic persons to health and strength, and wonderfully conducing in all cases of obstructions. There are good howses and accom'odation at reasonable rates." This property now belongs to W. H. Ludlow Bruges, Esq. M.P., of Seend, who preserves the well, but its waters are not resorted to for sanatory purposes. Other waters of similar quality at Melksham, in the vicinity of Seend, were formerly much used, and a pump-room and lodging houses were built around them ; but fashion, that fickle goddess, has not given them the fiat of her approval.

ACCIDENTS OF JOHN AUBREY.*

Born at Easton-Piers March 1625-6, about sun-rising ; very weak, and like to dye, and therefore christned that morning before prayer. I think I have heard my mother say I had an ague shortly after I was born.

1629. About three or four years old I had a grievous ague ; I can remember it. I got not health till eleven or twelve, but had sickness of vomiting for 12 hours every fortnight for . . . years, then it came monthly for . . . , then quarterly, and then half-yearly ; the last was in June 1642. This sickness nipt my strength in the bud.

1633. At eight years old I had an issue (naturall) in the coronall sutor of my head, which continued running till 21.

1634. October, I had a violent fevor, it was like to have carried me off ; 'twas the most dangerous sickness that ever I had.

1639. About 1639 or 1643 I had the measills, but that was nothing, I was hardly sick. Monday after Easter week my uncle's nag ranne away with me, and gave me a very dangerous fall.

1642. May 3, entered at Trinity College.

1643. April and May, the small pox at Oxon ; after left that ingeniouse place, and for three yeares led a sad life in the country.

1646. April . . admitted of the M. Temple ; but my father's sickness and business never permitted me to make any settlement to my study.

1651. About the 16 or 18 of April I sawe that incomparable good conditioned gentlewoman, Mrs. M. Wiseman, with whom at first sight I was in love.

1652. October the 21, my father died.

1655 (I think) June 14, I had a fall at Epsam, and brake one of my ribbes, and was afraid it might cause an apostumation.†

1656. Sept. 1655, or rather I think 1656, I began my chargeable and tedious lawe suite on the entaile in Brecknockshire and Monmouthshire. This yeare and the last was a strange yeare to me. Several love and lawe suites.

1656. . . . . Decemb. ☿ morb.

1657. Novemb. 27, obiit Dña Kasker Ryves, with whom I was to marry, to my great losse.

1659. March or April, like to break my neck in Ely Minster : and the next day, riding a gallop there, my horse tumbled over and over, and yet, I thank God, no hurt.

1660. July, Aug. I accompanied A. Ettrick into Ireland for a month, and returning, were like to be ship-wreckt at Holyhead, but no hurt done.

---

* This document has been printed, though somewhat imperfectly, in a work entitled *Oxoniana;* (4 vols, 12mo.) edited by the late Rev. J. Walker, of New College, Oxford.

† " APOSTUMATION, An abscess." [*Johnson.*] A prescription written for Aubrey by Dr. W. Harvey " to prevent an impostumation," and dated November 1655, is inserted in the collection of *Letters* from Aubrey's correspondents, in the *Ashmolean Museum* (vol. i.).

1661. ⎫ About these years I sold my estate in Herefordshire.

1662. ⎬

1663. ⎭ Janu.　I had the honour to be elected Fellow of the R. S.

1664. June 11, landed at Calais; in August following had a terrible fit of the spleen and piles at Orleans. I returned in October.

1664 or 1665. Munday after Christmas was in danger to be spoiled by my horse; and the same day received læsio in testiculo, which was like to have been fatal.　O. R. Wiesman quod—I believe 1664.

1665. November 1, I made my first address (in an ill hour) to Joane Sumner.*

1666. This year all my business and affairs ran kim kam, nothing tooke effect, as if I had been under an ill tongue.　Treacheries and enmities in abundance against me.

1667.　December . . . arrested in Chancery-lane, at Mrs. Sumner's suite.

Feb. 24, A.M., about 8 or 9. Triall with her at Sarum; victory and 600l. damaged; though devilish opposition against me.

1668. July 6, was arrested by Peter Gale's malicious contrivance the day before I was to go to Winton for my second triall; but it did not retard me above two hours, but did not then go to triall.

1669. March 5, was my triall at Winton from eight to nine.　The judge being exceedingly made against me by my Lady Hungerford, but four of the . . . . . . appearing, and much adoe, got the moiety of Sarum; verdict in 300l.

1669 and 1670. I sold all my estate in Wilts.　From 1670 to this very day (I thank God,) I have enjoyed a happy delitescency.

1671. . . . Danger of arrests.

1677. Latter end of June an impostume brake in my head.

Mdm. St. John's night, 1673, in danger of being run through with a sword by a young templer at Mr. Burges' chamber, in the M. Temple.

I was in danger of being killed by William Earl of Pembroke, then Lord Herbert, at the election of Sir William Salkeld for New Sarum.　I have been in danger of being drowned twice.

The year that I lay at Mr. Neve's (for a short time) I was in great danger of being killed by a drunkard in the street of Gray's Inn Gate by a gentleman whom I never saw before, but (Deo Gratias) one of his companions hindred his thrust.

> [1754. June 11, transcribed from a MS. in Mr. Aubrey's own hand-
> writing, in the possession of Dr. R. Rawlinson.]

Such are the auto-biographical memoranda of John Aubrey; and, although they are slight in texture, they afford a clear and vivid insight into the elements of a character which was unique, and contradistinguished from that of all his compeers.

* The manuscript in the Bodleian Library, in the hand-writing of Ballard, has the name here distinctly written "*Joane Brewer.*"　Dr. Rawlinson, however, quoting from the original, in Aubrey's writing, (then in his own possession), prints it "*Joane Sumner;*" and, as this reading is corroborated by subsequent passages, as well as by Aubrey's other memoranda, it is here corrected as a mere error of the transcriber, though it is certainly one of a most extraordinary kind.

As frequent reference will be made in the following memoir to Aubrey's various works, it is thought desirable to insert a list of them in this place. It is copied from the original in his own hand-writing at the end of the eleventh manuscript mentioned in the list; which, with most of the others, is preserved in the *Ashmolean Museum*. The list is headed "A Catalogue of Books written by Mr. Aubrey; inserted here by himself, at my request, Nov. 18, 1692. Edw. Lhwyd." Some of the manuscripts here mentioned are not now extant, viz. those numbered 5. 12. 13. 16. 18. 20. 21. and 22., but of these Nos. 5. 12. and 22. were probably cancelled on the publication of his *Miscellanies*, which elucidated the matters they seem to have referred to.

1. Antiquities of Wiltshire, after the method of Sir W. Dugdale's Description of Warwickshire. 2 parts in fol.

2. Monumenta Britannica. 3 parts fol. Wth Mr. Secretary Trumbull.

3. Memoires of Naturall Remarques in Wilts. 2 parts fol.

4. Perambulation of halfe the County of Surrey. Fol. With Mr. J. Evelyn.

5. Miscellanea. Fol.

6. Lives. 3 parts. . . . . .

7. Mr. Th. Hobbes' Life in English.

8. An Apparatus of the Lives of English Mathematicians. A q^r. At Gresham Colledge.

9. Idea of Education of Young Gentlemen from 9 to 18. Fol. The correct copie is wth Anthony Henley, Esq. at ye Grange, in Hampshire.

10. Remaines of Gentilisme. 3 parts, sc. about 3 q^{rs}. With Dr. Kennet.

11. Villare Anglicanum, [to be] interpreted. Fol.

12. A Collection of Divine Dreames from persons of my acquaintance, worthy of beliefe. 8vo.

13. Hypothesis Ethic & Scala Religionis. Wth Dr. Waple, Minister of Sepulchres by Newgate.

14. A Collection of Genitures well attested. 4to.

15. Easton Piers delineated.

16. Villa, or a Description of the Prospects from Easton Piers.

17. Faber Fortunæ, a private essay.

18. A Collection of Approved Receipts.

19. A Collection of Letters, writt to me from about 100 ingeniose persons inch $\frac{1}{2}$ thick. This I designe for the Musæum.

20. Adversaria Physica.

21. An Introduction to Architecture.

22. Some Strictures of Hermetick Philosophy, collected by J. Aubrey. Wth Dr. Waple.

Chap. II.

DESCENT AND PEDIGREE OF AUBREY—JOHN AUBREY'S BIRTH-PLACE—HIS INFANCY AND SCHOOL DAYS—
IS ENTERED AT TRINITY COLLEGE, OXFORD, AND THE MIDDLE TEMPLE—COMMENCEMENT OF
THE CIVIL WARS—DISCOVERY OF AVEBURY—HIS FATHER'S DEATH—HIS FIRST LITERARY WORKS
—A MEMBER OF A REPUBLICAN CLUB—JOURNEY TO IRELAND—INTERVIEW WITH CHARLES II. AT
AVEBURY AND SILBURY HILL—JOURNEY TO FRANCE—MATRIMONIAL PROJECTS.

AUBREY, or AUBERY, as a surname, is considered by Aubrey himself to class
with Godfrey, or Rowland, and many others, originally employed to designate
individuals, but afterwards used as family names.* Some writers† who have
noticed the ancestors of John Aubrey state that he "descended from Saunders de
St. Aubrey, or Alberic," a member of the royal family of France, who accompanied
William of Normandy in his successful invasion of England: and they further
narrate, with great show of accuracy, the establishment of the family in Brecknockshire, its alliance by marriage with a descendant of a monarch of South Wales, and
the consequent extension of its influence and importance in that ancient principality.
Without dwelling upon these or other points ‡ in the early history of the family,
which are undeniably involved in much obscurity, it will be sufficient for the purpose
of this memoir to observe that it was certainly of some consequence in the reign

* Aubrey's *Monumenta Britannica;* Rev. T. Delafield, in Kennett's *Parochial Antiquities,* ed. 1818,
vol. ii. p. 523 ; Camden's *Remains,* p. 58.

† See Betham's *Baronetage ;* Bowles's *History of Chalk Hundred,* in Hoare's *Modern Wilts ;* &c.

‡ The name "John Aubrey" occurs seven times in the *Hundred Rolls of Edward I.;* and in the
reign of Edward III. one "Andrew Aubrey" had a grant (*Pat. A° 27 E. III.*) of certain tenements in
London, which he held of the king, in capite. He was Lord Mayor of London in 1339, 1340, and 1351, and
on one occasion lent the king 800*l.* (*French Chronicle of London, Hen. III. to Edward III.,* printed by
the *Camden Society.*) One of the charges upon which the Lord Chancellor Bacon was disgraced and fined
was that he had accepted a bribe of 100*l.* from "Christopher Awbrey," a poor gentleman, who borrowed the
money of an Usurer, in order to secure a favourable judgment in a suit then pending before the Chancellor,
between himself and Sir William Bronker. (See *State Trials.*) It is probable that these individuals were
of the same family as the subject of this memoir, though their relationship cannot now be traced.

of Queen Elizabeth, when, in the person of Dr. William Aubrey, the name first became distinguished in science and law.

This eminent individual was born at Cantre in Brecknockshire, and studied the civil law at All Souls' College, Oxford. In this he attained great proficiency, taking his degree as Doctor at the age of twenty-five, and obtaining immediately afterwards the appointment of Regius Professor. He appears to have been warmly patronized by William, Earl of Pembroke, to whose family he was distantly related; for when the Earl commanded the English forces in France, Dr. Aubrey was his judge advo-cate, and a judge marshal of the royal army at St. Quintin's. On his return to England he practised with such fame and credit as an advocate of the court of Arches, that he was "accounted peerlesse in that facultie.*" He was successively appointed one of the Council of the Marches in Wales, a Master in Chancery, Official Principal and Vicar-General to his friend and patron, Whitgift, Archbishop of Canterbury, and, by the special favour of the Queen, who "loved him, and was wont to call him her *little doctor*," a Master of the Requests in ordinary. Dr. Aubrey was one of the delegates for the trial of Mary Queen of Scots, and was desirous to save her life; in acknowledgement of which James I. afterwards knighted his two eldest sons. He is highly spoken of in *Thuanus's Annales,* and in *Dr. Zouch's, De Jure Feciali:* his judicial decrees were quoted and acted on by Coke and Atkins, as of high authority. He had a country house at Kew, and lived on intimate terms with his relative and neighbour, Dr. Dee, the celebrated astrologer, of Mortlake. A curious certificate of Dr. Aubrey's funeral in St. Paul's Cathedral, signed by his three sons, and narrating fully his titles, alliances, and issue, is printed in Collins's *Baronetage,* vol. iii. p. 111 (1741). His monument was destroyed with the cathedral in the great fire of 1666.

It will be seen by the accompanying pedigree that John Aubrey, the antiquary, was descended from John, the youngest son of this distinguished man. His other sons, Sir Edward and Sir Thomas, inherited respectively the family estates in the counties of Brecknock and Glamorgan. The eldest branch soon became extinct, for

---

* See the notice from which this is abridged, in Aubrey's *Lives of Eminent Men,* in *Letters from the Bodleian,* vol. ii. pp. 207—221.

at the time of the Restoration, John Aubrey, of Llantrithyd, Glamorganshire, the son of Sir *Thomas* Aubrey, was the head of the family : and on the 23rd July, 1660, he was created a baronet by Charles II.,—the Aubreys having maintained a firm adherence to the royal cause. Sir John, the second baronet, added to his other estates that of Borstall, in Buckinghamshire,* which he acquired by marriage with the daughter and heiress of William Lewis, and from that time until recently, Borstall and Llantrithyd have been amongst the principal seats of the Aubrey family.† The old baronial mansion at Llantrithyd has however been suffered to fall into a truly lamentable and degrading state. The Rev. Dr. Ingram, of Oxford, wrote respecting it as follows, in 1837 : " Magnificent staircases, embossed and panelled ceilings, carved chimney-pieces, and armorial embellishments of the most splendid kind, are fast sinking into one common ruin. The roofs are falling, and it is scarcely safe to walk over the floors."‡ Of the once interesting mansion at Borstall, which was several times besieged during the Civil Wars, nothing now remains but a substantially built gateway, flanked by turrets at the angles. Some account of it, with a view of the Tower-Gateway, are given in Brayley's " Graphic and Historical Illustrator."

---

* This property was granted by Edward the Confessor to Nigel, a huntsman (who had slain a wild boar which infested the adjacent royal forest of Bernwood), "*per unum cornu, quod est charta prædictæ forestæ.*" The estate descended from Nigel by several heirs female to the family of Aubrey. The *Borstall horn*, well known to antiquaries, and an *ancient chartulary*, in which the incident here referred to is depicted, were exhibited to the Society of Antiquaries in 1773, through the kindness of Sir John (then Mr.) Aubrey, the 6th baronet, and they were by his permission engraved, and described, in the third volume of the *Archæologia.*

† Collins, Betham, &c. ut supra.

‡ *Memorials of Oxford,*—Jesus College.

PEDIGREE OF AUBREY AND LYTE.

From Aubrey's *MSS. at Oxford*; Aubrey's *Lives of Eminent Men*, vol. ii. p. 219; *the Parish Registers of Kington St. Michael*; MSS. by Jas. Gilpin, *Recorder of Oxford*, 1756 *(in Ashm. Mus..)*; Bowles's *History of Chalk Hundred*; Betham's *Baronetage*, &c.

WILLIAM AUBREY, D.C.L., Regius Professor, Oxford; born about 1529, died 25 June 1595. = Wilgiford, dau. of John Williams, esq. of Teynton, Oxon. = ... Browne, esq. of Willey, Surrey; 2nd husb. — Thomas Lyte, of Easton Pierse, Wilts, born 1531, died May, 1627, bur. at Kington St. Michael. = Eleanor, dau. of Isaac Taylor, of Kington Priory, Wilts; marr. Dec. 7, 1568, died Jan. 29, 1582.

SIR EDWARD AUBREY, of Brecknockshire. = Joan, dau. of Wm. Havard, esq. of Brecknockshire. | SIR THOMAS AUBREY, of Glamorganshire. = Mary, d. & h. of Anthony Mansell, esq. of Llantrithyd, Glamorganshire. | JOHN AUBREY, of Burleton, Herefordshire. = Rachel, dau. of Richard Danvers, esq. of Tokenham, Wilts; d. 1656. = John Whitson, Alderman of Bristol, b. 1557, d. Mar. 1629; 2d husb. | Elizabeth. Mary. Joan. Wilgiford. Lucy. Anne. All married. | Isaac Lyte, of Easton-Pierse born 19 Mar. 1576, died 21 Feb. 1659; bur. at Kington. = Israel, dau. of Thos. Browne, of Winterbourne Basset, Wilts, b. 1578, d. 24 Feb. 1662, bur. at Kington.

7 sons, and 5 daughters. | SIR JOHN AUBREY, 1st Bart. = Mary, dau. and heiress of —— South. | Thomas Aubrey, marr. A. Rudd. | 3 Daughters. | RICHARD AUBREY, of Burleton, Herefordsh. and Broad Chalk, Wilts; born 1603, died at Broad Chalk, 21st, and bur. at Kington 26th Oct. 1652. = Deborah, dau. and heiress, born Jan. 1610, marr. 15 June 1625, died at Broad Chalk 19th, and bu. at Kington, 25th April, 1686.

Lewis, died s. p. | Margaret Lowther, dau. of John 1st Lord Lonsdale. = SIR JOHN AUBREY, 2d Bart.; died Sept. 1700. = Mary, dau. and heiress of William Lewis, esq. of Borstall. | Mary, marr. W. Montague, Lord Chief Baron of the Exchequer. Elizabeth, marr. Ralph Freeman, esq. | JOHN AUBREY, F.R.S., born at Easton-Pierse, Wilts, 12th March 1626; died at Oxford, unmarr. June 1697, bur. (June 7) at St. Mary Magdalene's church, Oxford. WILLIAM AUBREY, LL.B. Fellow of New College, Oxford, born 2nd Mar. 1643, died Oct. 1707, s. p. THOMAS AUBREY, born at Broad Chalk, Wilts, 1645; died unmarr. 15th Aug. 1681, buried at Broad Chalk. | Anne, bapt. at Kington, 23 June, 1628. | Isaac, bapt. 29th Jan., bur. 31st Jan. 1630, at Kington. Isaac, bapt. 22d Mar. 1631, bur. 22d Oct. 1632, at Kington.

Mary Staley, 1st wife. = SIR JOHN AUBREY, 3rd Baronet, died April 1743. = Frances Jephson, 2nd wife. = Jane Thomas, 3d wife.

SIR JOHN AUBREY, 4th Bart.; died unmarried, 14th Oct. 1767. | SIR THOMAS AUBREY, 5th Bart.; died 4 Sept. 1786. = Martha, dau. of Richard Carter, esq. of Chilton, Bucks, died 1788. | Mary, died unmarr. 1768. | Henry Lintot, esq. = Elizabeth, died Jan. 1734. | Frances, died 1775; marr. Denham Jephson, esq. | Margaret, died unmarried, 1793.

Mary, dau. of Sir James Colebrooke, Bart.; 1st wife. = SIR JOHN AUBREY, 6th Bart.; died 1st March 1826, bur. at Borstall, Bucks. = Martha-Catharine, dau. of George Richard Carter, esq. of Chilton; 2nd wife. | Thomas Aubrey, a Major in the Army; died 1814. | RICHARD AUBREY, Col. of the Glamorganshire Militia; marr. 26 Feb. 1780, died 1808. = Frances, dau. of the Hon. Wriothesley Digby. | Patty-Mary, d. unmarr. 1774.

John Aubrey, died young. | W. R. Cartwright, esq. M.P. = Julia-Frances. | SIR THOMAS DIGBY AUBREY, 7th Bart.; marr. 9th Dec. 1813. = Mary, dau. of Thomas Wright, esq. niece of the Rev. Robert Verney, of Middle Clayton, Bucks; died without issue, 1817.

John Aubrey, the youngest son of Dr. William Aubrey, and grandfather of the subject of this memoir, is mentioned in the private *Diary of Dr. Dee* (p. 52), published by the Camden Society. On his father's death he was left to the guardianship of Archbishop Whitgift, and, when about 18 years of age,* he married Rachel Danvers, a member of a Wiltshire noble family, and settled at Burleton, near Stretton, in Herefordshire. There, in 1603, his son Richard was born, who was married in his twenty-second year, in the parish church of Kington St. Michael, to Deborah, the only child of Isaac Lyte, of Easton-Pierse, in the same parish, she being then 15 years and six months old ;† and on the 12th of the succeeding month of March (1625-6) † their son, JOHN AUBREY, the future antiquary and topographer, was born, at Easton-Pierse.

His baptism, on the day of his birth, is duly recorded in the register of his native parish ; and he informs us that Alderman Whitson of Bristol, who had married his grandfather's widow, was his godfather ‡ In his *Description of the North Division of Wiltshire* Aubrey thus mentions the place of his birth :—" When my [great-]grandfather Thomas Lyte sold the mannor howse, with the lands near it, he built the howse on the browe of the hill above the brooke facing the south-east, from whence there is a lovely prospect. Here, in my grandfather's chamber (where in an ill hour I first drew my breath, ♄ [Saturn] directly opposing my ascendant), in the chimney, are these two escutcheons, [1. Gules, a chev. between three swans argent, a mullet sable for difference ; 2. An eagle displayed sable, legged gules, on its breast a crescent or.] Over the first shield is ' Isaac Lyte, natus 1576 ; ' over the second ' Israel Lyte.' It was built the same year my g^d father was born." In his *Designatio de Easton Pierse,* Aubrey gives some views of the house thus mentioned, from one of which the engraving in the title-page of the present work has been copied.§

It is evident from the passage here quoted that the farm-house known by the appellation of *Lower Easton-Pierse* was the place of Aubrey's nativity. Within

* *Life of Dr. W. Aubrey* above referred to.

† *Ibid.* and Aubrey's *Collection of Genitures,* and other *MSS. at Oxford.*

‡ *Lives of Eminent Men,* vol. ii. p. 477.

§ In one of the chamber windows represented in the wood-cut is the mark ⚥, indicating, as Aubrey says, " My grandfather Lyte's chamber, wherein I drew my first breath."

my recollection, which extends as far back as about 1780, there were many rooms
in that house, in one of which were several pieces of old armour, and other characteristics of an ancient mansion. These have all been swept away, and a modern
building erected on the site.

The "strong and early impulse to antiquities" which Aubrey felt, is doubtless
mainly attributable to the influence exerted on his youthful mind by the historical and
traditionary lore which he derived from the progenitors of his parents, and from other
old persons with whom he associated in infancy; for with such persons he "loved to
converse, as living histories." He occasionally resided with his paternal grandmother, and her second husband, Alderman Whitson,* not only in Bristol, but at
Burnet, in Somersetshire, which was the lady's jointure; and it was during his visits
to the latter place that Aubrey became acquainted with the neighbouring druidical
monument at Stanton Drew. As early as his eighth year, he tells us, he was
familiar with Stonehenge.†

He distinctly says that he was "bred at Eston (in Eremeticall solitude)," and there
he derived from old Isaac and Israel Lyte, and from several of the neighbouring
farmers, many local anecdotes, which his memory treasured up, and which he has
recorded, acknowledging their source, in his *Wiltshire Manuscripts*, and in his
Lives. Of Mrs. Lyte, his grandmother, who lived until his thirty-fifth year, Aubrey
always speaks with affectionate reverence, and it was his intention, "in duty to the
memory of her tenderness and dilligence in his education," to raise in Kington

* The natives of Bristol have good reason to hold in lasting reverence the name of this charitable and
noble-minded man, whose deeds in truth deserve a more than local fame. From a state of poverty John
Whitson rose, by his own industry and perseverance, till he became the wealthiest merchant of the city. He
was twice Mayor of Bristol, and represented it in four Parliaments. He was remarkable not only for his
piety and integrity, but for local patriotism, as well as for enlarged and liberal views of national policy. When
Rachel Aubrey became his third wife he had reached the summit of his prosperity, and by his Will, which,
with the exception of a provision for herself, bequeathed his property entirely to charitable uses, he appointed
her his sole executrix. Property to the amount of more than £300 per annum (then a large sum) was by
this will appropriated to the foundation and support of various schools, almshouses, &c. in Bristol. Amongst the
widow's charges about his funeral is the item to "M. Aubrey et uxor £20." John Whitson wrote a *Pious
Meditation, or Farewell to the World*, which, with some biographical notices of him, was reprinted in 1829
(8vo. Bristol). Whitson died in 1629, in his 72d year.

† *Monumenta Britannica.*

Church a tablet, with a longer inscription than that which had been placed there at the time of her interment.*

The following are some of Aubrey's reminiscences of boyhood. In 1633 he "entred into his Grammar at the Latin schoole at Yatton Keynel,† in the church, where the Curate, Mr. Hart, taught the eldest boyes Virgil, Ovid, Cicero, &c." He adds, "The fashion then was to save the forules of their bookes with a false cover of parchment, si. old manuscript, which I was too young to understand; but I was pleased with the elegancy of the writing and the coloured initiall letters. I remember the Rector (Mr. William Stump, great gr. son ‡ of St: the cloathier of Malmesbury) had severall manuscripts of the abbey. He was a proper man, and a good fellow, and when he brewed a barrell of special ale his use was to stop the bunghole (under the clay) with a sheet of manuscript. He sayd nothing did it so well, which me thought did grieve me then to see."§ In the next year, 1634, Aubrey was placed under Mr. Robert Latimer, Rector of Leigh-de-la-Mere, an adjoining parish, of whom he says incidentally, "I remember my old schoolmaster, Mr. Latimer, at 70, wore a dudgeon, with a knife, and bodkin, as also my old grandfather, Lyte, and Alderman Whitson of Bristowe, wch I suppose was the common fashion in their young dayes."‖ Thos. Hobbes, the philosopher of Malmesbury, had previously been under the tuition of Mr. Latimer, and, in a visit to his old preceptor, he first took notice of young Aubrey. The latter thus mentions the circumstance: "This summer, 1634 (I remember it was in venison season, July or Aug.), Mr. T. H. came into his native country to visitt his friends, and amongst others he came to see his old schoolmaster, Mr. Rob. Latimer,¶ at Leigh-de-la-Mere, when I was then a little youth at school, in

* *North Division of Wiltshire.*

† Here his grandfather Lyte had been a boy at school, when Camden visited and took notes in the church. Original letter from Aubrey to Wood, *in the Ballard Collection of Original Letters, in the Bodleian Library,* vol. xiv.

‡ He was descended probably from a *brother* of the rich clothier; of whose own descendants a pedigree may be seen in Collectanea Topogr. et Geneal. vol. vii. p. 83, 1841.

§ *Natural History of Wilts,* Chap. on *Worthies.* In 1798 I visited a farmer at Charlton, near Malmesbury, named Stump, who had some curious manuscripts, and several large folio volumes, in an old chest. These were probably the remains of the spoil which passed, with the manor and abbatial edifices of Malmesbury, to his ancestor Stump, the clothier.

‖ *Lives of Eminent Men,* vol. ii. p. 382.   ¶ " Rob. Latimer, obiit Nov. 2, 1634."

the church, newly entered into my grammar by him. Here was the first place and time that I ever had the honour to see this worthy, learned man, who was then pleased to take notice of me, and the next day came and visited my relations. He was a proper man, briske, and in very good equipage; his haire was then quite black. He stayed at Malmesbury, and in the neighbourhood, a weeke or better; 'twas the last time that ever he was in Wiltshire."* From this casual circumstance an intercourse commenced between Hobbes and Aubrey, which continued without interruption till the death of the former in 1679, and which was characterized by frank and liberal kindness on the one hand, and respectful deference on the other.

Aubrey informs us "there was the like use of covering of bookes" at Mr. Latimer's school. "In my grandfather's dayes," he says, "the manuscripts flew about like butterflies. All musick bookes, account bookes, copie bookes, &c. were covered with old manuscripts, as wee cover them now with blew paper or marbled paper; and the glovers at Malmesbury made great havock of them, and gloves were wrapt up no doubt in many good pieces of antiquity." †

For the next two or three years ill health, and study under "dull, ignorant teachers," doubtless retarded his school education, but on gaining strength, in 1638, he was "transplanted to Blandford schoole in Dorset, to Mr. Wm. Sutton." This he states was "in Mr. Wm. Gardner's time the most eminent schoole for the education of gentlemen in the West of England." ‡ Here he formed a lasting friendship with Mr. William Browne, B.D., an usher in the school. That gentleman was a son of the Rector of Churchill, Dorsetshire, and had himself been educated at Blandford, under Mr. Gardner. He frequently afterwards corresponded with Aubrey, who in mentioning his burial at Farnham, in Surrey, observes that "he was an ingenious man, a good scholar, and as admirable a disputant as any was in his time in the University. . . . . . It was my happiness to be his pupil." §

Of Aubrey's school days there are other notices scattered throughout his writings,

* *Life of Hobbes*, in *Letters from the Bodleian*, vol. ii. p. 604.

† *Natural Hist. of Wilts*, Chap. on *Worthies*. When at school I remember to have seen bibles, testaments, and some school books, covered with ancient writings on parchment. I also remember having learnt the alphabet from a *hornbook*: now extinct.

‡ *Ibid.*   § *History of Surrey*, vol. iii. p. 335.

but they are not of much importance, though they serve to shew the interest he felt, even at that early age, in matters of history and antiquity. He was at Gloucester with his father when he was nine years old,* and probably at Burleton, in Herefordshire, at an equally early date.

On the 2d of May, 1642, being then in his seventeenth year, he was entered as a gentleman-commoner of Trinity College, Oxford,† which college was probably selected as that to which his friend and tutor, Browne, belonged. In an old collection of caution-books preserved at Trinity College by the care of Dr. Bathurst, after the havoc made by the Parliamentary visitors, and now bound in one thick volume, quarto, there is an entry of £3 received in the year 1642, as a cautionary deposit from John Aubrey : " à *Johanne Aubrey*, 3£." The name is repeated, with the same sum annexed, in the annual accounts officially transferred to the Bursars in succession, till the year 1645. The confusion of the times occasioned a chasm in the accounts for nearly twenty years from this date, but there seems to be no reason to suppose that his name was removed from the college books.‡

Aubrey's memoir of Dr. Kettle § affords some curious illustrations of his college life ; and in his *Miscellanies* he says, "When I was a freshman at Oxford, in 1642, I was wont to go to Christchurch, to see King Charles I. at supper, where I once heard him say 'that as he was hawking in Scotland, he rode into the quarry, and found the covey of partridges falling upon the hawk ;' and I do remember this expression further, viz. 'and I will swear upon the book 'tis true.' When I came to my chamber, I told this story to my tutor ; said he, that covey was London."‖

Aubrey's first stay at Oxford was short. The anticipated hostilities between the King and Parliament induced his parents to remove him for a time from the University. He himself says, " The first brush was between the Earl of Northampton and the Lord Brooke, neer Banbury, which was the latter end of July, or the beginning of August, 1642. I was sent for [from Oxford] into the country, to my great griefe,

* See *Lives of Eminent Men*, vol. ii. p. 554, where he mentions a curious picture of the funeral of Sir Philip Sidney which he saw at Gloucester, and which, he says, "made such a strong impression on my young tender phantasy, that I remember it as if it were but yesterday."

† *Aubrey's MSS. at Oxford.*   ‡ Communicated by the Rev. Dr. Ingram.

§ *Lives of Eminent Men*, vol. ii. p. 417.   ‖ *Miscellanies*, Chap. on *Omens*.

and departed the 9th of Aug.; 'twas before I went away." *　It is probable that on leaving Oxford, at this time, Aubrey went to Broad Chalk, in Wiltshire, where his father had become lessee of the Manor Farm, under the Earl of Pembroke.　He thus mentions Chalk as early as 1643: "Major John Morgan fell sick of a malignant fever as he was marching with the King's army into the West, and was brought to my father's at Broad Chalk, where he was lodged secretly in a garret." †　Browne's letters to him about this time, with those of other correspondents, are addressed to "his father's house at Broad Chalk." ‡

On the 16th of April 1646, Aubrey was admitted a student of the Middle Temple; but he distinctly states that "his father's sickness and business never permitted him to make any settlement to his study."

In January 1649 he discovered the remains of the great Druidical Temple at Avebury, in Wiltshire; an event which he thus describes: "I never saw the country about Marleborough till Christmas 1648, being then invited to Lord Francis Seymour's, by the Honourable Mr. Charles Seymour, with whom I had the honour to be intimately acquainted, and whose friendship I ought to mention with a profound respect to his memorie.　The morrow after twelf-day Mr. Charles Seymour and Sir William Button met with their packs of hounds at the Grey Wethers.　These downes looke as if they were sowen with great stones, very thick, and in a dusky evening they looke like a flock of sheep, from whence they take their name: one might fancy it to have been the scene where the giants fought with huge stones against the gods.§ . . . . 'Twas here that our game began, and the chase led us at length thorough the village of Aubury into the closes there, where I was wonderfully surprised at the sight of those vast stones, of which I had never heard before, as also

---

* *Lives of Eminent Men*, vol. ii. p. 295.

† *Miscellanies*, Chap. on *Omens*.　The attachment of John Aubrey and others of his family to the royal cause is shown by many scattered passages in his papers, wherein "the Puritan faction" are severely stigmatized.　His private diaries, if preserved, would doubtless have added much interesting matter to the records of that eventful period.　The estate of his cousin, Sir John Aubrey, the first Baronet, at Llantrithyd, was sequestrated by the Parliament, and Leoline (afterwards Judge) Jenkins became tutor to several Welsh gentlemen of quality in the house, whilst it remained unoccupied by the Aubrey family.—*Wood's Fasti*, part ii. p. 231.

‡ Originals in a *Coll. of Letters to Aubrey* in the *Ashmolean Museum*.

§ The Grey Wethers are described in the *Beauties of Wiltshire*, vol. iii. and in Hoare's *Ancient Wiltshire*, vol. ii.

at the mighty bank and graffe about it. I observed in the enclosures some segments of rude circles made with these stones, whence I concluded they had been in the old time complete. I left my company awhile, entertaining myself with a more delightful indagation,* and then, (cheered by the cry of the hounds,) overtook the company, and went with them to Kynnet, where was a good hunting dinner provided."†

In the same year Aubrey was collecting information respecting the mysterious noises which disturbed the Parliamentary Commissioners at Woodstock;‡ and we find that in 1651 he witnessed the execution of Christopher Love, on Tower Hill, on a charge of high-treason. "I did see Mr. Christopher Love beheaded on Tower Hill in a delicate clear day; about half an hour after his head was struck off the clouds gathered blacker and blacker, and such terrible claps of thunder came, that I never heard greater."—*Miscellanies*, Chap. on *Omens*. This was on the 22nd of August.§ The superstition here countenanced by Aubrey was implicitly believed by the inhabitants of Kington St. Michael seventy years ago; when a thunder storm, occurring immediately after the execution of a murderer near the parish, was regarded as a special indication of Divine anger. No doubt the same credulity still prevails in many parts of England.

With reference to this period of his life, he says, in his Memoir of Dr. William Harvey, "I had not the honour to be acquainted with him till 1651, being my cos. Montagu's ‖ physitian and friend. I was at that time bound for Italy (but to my great

* "INDAGATION, Search, inquiry, examination." *Boyle*, cited in *Johnson's Dictionary*.

† *Monumenta Britannica:* (and see Hoare's *Ancient Wiltshire*, vol. ii. p. 58, where the entire passage is quoted.)

‡ See a *Letter* in the *Ashmolean Museum* addressed to him on this subject by J. Lyddall, dated 11th March, 1649, and printed by Aubrey in his *Miscellanies.* The same topic has afforded Sir Walter Scott the groundwork for his interesting romance of *Woodstock.* Sir Henry Lee of Ditchley, who figures so prominently in that work, married the daughter of Sir John Danvers, and was therefore distantly allied to the family of Aubrey. Moreover, his son-in-law, the Earl of Abingdon, was a friend and patron of John Aubrey. These circumstances may account for Aubrey's feeling much interest in the events relating to Woodstock. The "invisible drummer" who haunted the manor-house of North Tidworth, Wilts, about twelve years afterwards, equally excited the alarm of the whole neighbourhood, and gave rise to numerous conjectures. Addison wrote a comedy on the subject, called "The Drummer, or the Haunted House."

§ Love's principal offence was holding communication with the exiled Charles the Second: he made a very long address to the populace before he was beheaded, and met his fate with fortitude. John Gibbons suffered on the same scaffold, immediately after him.—Cobbett's *State Trials*, vol. v.

‖ Montague Bertie, afterwards second Earl of Abingdon.

grief dissuaded by my mother's importunity). He was very communicative, and in order to my journey, dictated to me what to see, what company to keep, what bookes to read, how to manage my studies." *

His mother's importunities were caused, there is little doubt, by the illness of his father, who for nearly two years appears to have been gradually sinking. He died on the 21st of October 1652, at Broad Chalk, and was buried on the 26th at Kington St. Michael.† In his account of that Church, Aubrey says, "In the south-east corner lieth the body of my Father, under a stone thus inscribed, and now almost out : 'HIC JACET QUOD RELIQUUM EST RICHARDI AWBREY ARMIGERI, QUI OBIIT 21 DIE MENSIS OCTOBRIS, MDCLII.' "‡

It does not appear that Richard Aubrey sympathised with his son's pursuits, as indeed may be inferred from the preceding auto-biography. Upon his death John inherited the farm at Broad Chalk, where he now chiefly resided, and also the manor of Burleton, in Herefordshire. The house at Easton-Pierse, in which he was born, was probably still occupied by his mother's parents, Isaac and Israel Lyte.

In 1655 Inigo Jones's volume on *Stonehenge*, in which the author attributed that Temple to the Romans, was published by his son-in-law, John Webb ; upon which work Aubrey properly observes, " There is a great deal of learning in it, but, having compared his scheme [i. e. plan] with the monument itself, I found he had not dealt fairly, but had made a Lesbian's rule, which is conformed to the stone ; that is, he framed the monument to his own hypothesis, which is much differing from the thing itself ; and this gave me an edge to make more researches, and a further opportunity was, that my honoured and faithfull friend, Colonel James Long, of Draycot, was wont to spend a week or two every autumne at Aubury in hawking, where several times I have had the happiness to accompany him. Our sport was

---

* *Lives of Eminent Men*, vol. ii. p. 382.

† *Parish Register, Kington St. Michael.* "Three or four days before my father died I did hear three distinct knocks on the bed's head."—Aubrey's *Miscellanies*, Chap. on *Knockings*.

‡ *North Division of Wiltshire.* He also says, " My father and mother are buried in the south-east angle of the chancell. I do hope to live so long to erect a little inscription of white marble to the memory of my father about an ell high or better. ' P. M. Richardi Awbrey Armig. filii unici Johannis Awbrey de Burlton in agro Heref. filii tertii Gulielmi Awbrey LL.D. et e supplicum libellis Eliz. Reg. Magri. Viri pacifici & fidelis amici. Uxorem duxit Deborah filiam et heredem Isaaci Lyte de Easton Pierse, per quam suscepit tres superstites, Johannem, Gulielmum, et Thomam, filios. Obiit xxi die Oct. Ano Dni. 1652, Ætat. 49.' "

very good, and in a romantick countrey, for the prospects are noble and vast, the downs stockt with numerous flocks of sheep, the turfe rich and fragrant with thyme and burnet,—

' Fessus ubi incubuit baculo, saxoque resedit
      Pastor arundineo carmine mulcet oves;'

nor are the nut-brown shepherdesses without their graces. But the flight of the falcons was but a parenthesis to the Colonell's facetious discourse, who was 'tam Marti quam Mercurio,' and the Muses did accompany him with his hawkes and spaniells."*

In 1656 Aubrey began the *Natural History of Wiltshire*,† his first literary work, some account of which, and of his other manuscripts, will be given at the end of this memoir.

Excepting the following testamentary document in John Aubrey's handwriting, which belongs to this period of his life, we have only two or three trivial notices of him between 1656 and 1659.‡ The directions in this paper for a monument to his father fixes it as later than 1652; and, as his grandfather, Isaac Lyte, is named in it as living, it must have been written prior to 1659, in which year the latter died.

DRAUGHT OF MY WILL.

To my loving grandfather, Mr. Isaac Lyte, 50 li. and to my grandmother, 50 li. A decent inscription of white marble for my father, and yᵉ like for my selfe; yᵉ Epitaph to be made by Mr. A. Ettrick.

Itᵐ, to Anthony Ettrick, of Berford, in yᵉ county of Dorset, esq., I bequeath ten pounds to buy a piece of plate, my saphire ring, Sʳ Walter Raleigh's history, and Philip Comineus.

Itᵐ, my will is that my Executors buy for Trinity College in Oxon. a colledge pott

---

* *Monumenta Britannica*, ut supra. It is highly creditable to Aubrey's knowledge of drawing, particularly of ground-plans, to have detected the misrepresentations of Jones, who, to prop a silly hypothesis, not only altered in his plan the positions of many of the stones which formed the temple of Stonehenge, but added others to their number.

† Now in the *Ashmolean Museum, Oxford*. A fair copy of it by Aubrey is also in the *Library of the Royal Society, London*.

‡ "I heard Oliver Cromwell, Protector (at dinner at Hampton Court, 1657 or 8) tell the Lord Arundell of Wardour and the Lord FitzWilliams that he had been in all the counties of England, and that the Devonshire husbandry was the best."—Aubrey's *Natural Hist. of Wilts*, Chap. on *Agriculture*.

of the value of ten pounds, wth my arms thereon inscribed, and ten pounds wch I shall desire my honored friend Mr. Ralph Bathurst of Trinity College, and Mr. Jo. Lydall, to lay out upon Mathematicall and Philosophicall books.

It^{m}, I give to the library of Jesus Colledge in Oxon, my greeke Crysostoms, Bedes, 2 tomes, and all the rest of my bookes that are fitt for ye library, as Mr. Anthony Ettrick or Mr. John Lydall shall think fitt, excepting those bookes that were my father's, which I bequeath to my heire.

It^{m}, I bequeath to John Davenant of ye Middle Temple esq. a ring of ye value of 50s. wth a stone in it."   [The like bequest follows to Mr. William Hawes of Trinity College, and to his friends John Lydall, and Ralph Bathurst.]

It^{m}, to M^{ris} Mary Wiseman of Westminster my best diamond ring and . . ."*

———————

In 1659 Aubrey commenced a second work relating to Wiltshire, under peculiar and interesting circumstances. It was intended to form part of a *County History*, as that term is now understood; and other portions were to have been undertaken by gentlemen of equal learning and ability: constituting in fact the first "TOPOGRAPHICAL SOCIETY" on record. Aubrey terms this work "An Essay towards the Description of the *North Division* of Wiltshire," and in an Introduction to it he thus writes: " At a meeting of gentlemen at the Devizes for choosing of Knights of the Shire in March 1659, it was wish'd by some that this county (wherein are many observable antiquities) was survey'd, in imitation of Mr. Dugdale's Illustration of Warwickshire;† but it being too great a task for one man, Mr. William Yorke, (Councellor at Law, and a lover of this kind of learning,) advis'd to have the labour divided; he himself would undertake the Middle Division, I would undertake the North ; T. Gore, Esq. Jeffrey Daniel, Esq. and Sir John Erneley, would be assistants.‡" The valuable collections, illustrating the topography of North Wiltshire, which Aubrey made in pursuance of this arrangement, remain a lasting proof

———————

* *Original* in the *Ashmolean Museum*, Oxford. Of the parties mentioned in this document Hawes and Bathurst both became afterwards Presidents of Trinity College, and Lydall Warden of Merton.

† Dugdale's *Warwickshire* was first published in one volume, folio, 1656.

‡ *Original* in the *Ashmolean Museum*, Oxford. This Introduction is dated " Eston-Pierse, April 28th, 1670," long after the project had been first discussed.

of his ability, industry, and zeal in a good cause. Parts of these have been printed
and published by Sir Thomas Phillipps, Bart. (ante, p. 2.) ; but it is to be regretted
that the task has not been more successfully performed, for the printed work gives
but an imperfect idea of the original manuscript. The latter has a great number of
plans, views, and other drawings, by Aubrey ; all the armorial shields referred to are
elaborately emblazoned ; the ancient deeds quoted are copied as *fac-similes* of the
originals, with drawings of the seals, and the whole may be regarded as the most
curious work of its kind then extant.

In 1659 Aubrey was Churchwarden of Broad Chalk, as still indicated by the
following inscription : " This church was repaired, the four bells changed to six,
anno 1659. George Penruddock and John Aubrey, Esqrs. Churchwardens." These
bells remain in the tower. The Penruddocks were lessees of the Broad Chalk farm
before it was held by the Aubreys.*

In the same year he became a member of a celebrated club which met to discuss
the principles of government, and which he thus mentions in his Memoir of JAMES
HARRINGTON, author of the then popular *Oceana*. He states that Harrington
"made severall essayes in poetry, but his muse was rough ; and Mr. Henry Nevill,
an ingeniose and well-bred gent., a member of the H. of Commons, and an excellent
(but concealed) poet, was his great familiar and confident friend, and dissuaded
him from tampering with poetrie, which he did, *invitâ Minervâ*, and to improve his
proper talent, viz. political reflections. Whereupon he writ his *Oceana*, printed,
London . . . . . Mr. Hobbes was wont to say that H. Nevil had a finger in yᵉ pye,
and 'tis like enough. That ingeniose tractat, together with his and H. Nevill's
smart discourses and inculcations dayly at coffee-houses, made many proselytes. In
so much that Aᵒ 1659, the beginning of Michaelmas-term, he had every night a
meeting at the (then) Turkes head, in the New Pallace-Yard, where they take water,
the next house to the staires, at one Miles's, where was made purposely a large
ovall-table, with a passage in the middle for Miles to deliver his coffee. About it sate
his disciples, and the virtuosi. The discourses in this kind were the most ingeniose
and smart that ever I heard, or expect to hear, and larded with great eagernesse ;

* Bowles's *History of Chalk Hundred*, in Hoare's *Modern Wiltshire*, pp. 133, 151.

the arguments in the Parl. house were but flatt to it. He now printed a little
pamphlet called the *Rota*, 4to.   Here we had (very formally) a *ballotting-box*, and
ballotted how things should be carried, by way of Tentamens. The room was every
evening full as it could be crammed. I cannot now recount the whole number ;
Mr. Cyriack Skinner, an ingeniose young gent., scholar to Jo. Milton, was chaireman. There was Mr. Hen. Nevill, Major Wildman, Mr. . . . . Wooseley, of . . . ,
Staffordsh., Mr. Coke, gr. son of Sir Edw., Sir William Poulteney (Chaireman), Mr.
Maximilian Petty (a very able man in these matters, and who had more than once
turned the councill-board of O. Cromwell, his kinsman) ; Mr. Michael Malett, Mr.
. . . . Carteret, of Garnely, ... Cradoc, a merchant, Mr. Hen. Ford, Major
Verner, Mr. Edward Bagshaw, ... Croon, M.D., *cum multis aliis*, now slipt out of
my memorie, which were as auditors as myselfe.   Severall, *e. g.* yᵉ Earle Tirconnel,
Sʳ John Penruddock, &c. Mr. Jo. Birkenhead, ... Stafford, Esq. &c. opponents.
Several soldiers (officers). We many times adjourned to the Rhenish wine house.
One time, Mr. Stafford, and his gang, came in drunk from the taverne, and affronted
the junto ; the soldiers offered to kick them downe stayres, but Mr. Harrington's
moderation and persuasion hindered it.   Mr. Stafford tore their orders and minutes.
The doctrine was very taking ; and the more because, as to human foresight, there
was no possibility of the King's returne.   But the greatest part of the Parliament-
men perfectly hated this designe of *rotation by ballotting*, for they were cursed
tyrants, and in love with their power, and 'twas death to them, except 8 or 10,
to admitt of this way, for H. Nevill proposed it in the House, and made it out to
them that except they embraced that modell of government they would be ruined ;
sed quos perdere vult Jupiter, hos, &c.   Pride of senators for life is insufferable ; and
they were able to grind any one they owed ill will to powder ; they were hated by
the armie, and their country they represented, and their name and memorie stinkes.
'Twas worse than tyranny. Now this modell upon rotation was that the third part
of the House should rote out by ballot every yeare, so that every ninth yeare the
House would be wholly altered. No magistrate to continue above 3 yeares, and all
to be chosen by ballot, than which manner of choice nothing can be invented more
fair and impartiall. Well ; this meeting continued Novemb., Dec., Jan., till Feb. 20

or 21, and then, upon the unexpected turne upon Generall Monke's comeing in, all these airie modells vanished.   Then 'twas not fitt, nay treason, to have donne such ; but I well remember he [Harrington] severall times (at the breaking up) sayd, 'Well, the King will come in.   Let him come in, and call a Parliament of ye great cavaliers in England, so they be men of estates, and let them sett but 7 yeares, and they will all turn Commonwealthes men.'"*

The arrival of General Monk in London, and the public events which ensued, are described by Aubrey in his interesting memoir of that individual.   On the 23rd July, 1660, Sir John Aubrey of Llantrithyd, was created a Baronet by King Charles II.   In the same month Aubrey accompanied his friend, Anthony Ettrick, to Ireland, and on returning in August they narrowly escaped shipwreck.   About twelve months afterwards he thus wrote to Thomas Hobbes : " From N. Wales I went into Ireland, where I saw the manner of living of the natives, scorning industry and luxury, contenting themselves only with things necessary.   That king-dom is in a very great distemper, and hath need of your advice to settle it ; the animosities between the English and Irish are very great, and will ere long, I am confident, break into a war.   Sir, you have done me so much honour in your acquaintance and civilities, that I want language to expresse my thankfulnesse ; among other favours I particularly return you my hearty thankes for the trouble I gave you to sitt for your picture,† which is an honour I am not worthy of, and I beg your pardon for my great boldness, but I assure you no man living more prizes it, nor hath greater devotion for you then myselfe.   Your brother I heare is well,

---

* *Lives of Eminent Men*, vol. ii. p. 371.   See also the same passage, with alterations and additions by Wood, in *Athen. Oxon.* (Life of Harrington.)

† In Aubrey's *Life of Hobbes* (*Lives of Eminent Men*, vol. ii. p. 632,) he says: " He did me the honour to sitt for his picture to Jo. Baptist Caspars, an excellent painter, and 'tis a good piece.   I presented it to the [Royal] Societie twelve yeares since."   It appears by a letter from Hollar to Aubrey, in the Ashmolean Museum (dated in 1665), that the former engraved a portrait of Hobbes from a picture lent to him by Aubrey: no doubt the picture by Caspars here alluded to.   Aubrey also mentions another portrait of Hobbes (*Lives*, vol. ii. p. 610).   " Mr. Samuel Cowper, the prince of limners of this last age, drew his picture as like as art could afford, and one of the best pieces that ever he did, which his Majesty (Chas. II.) at his returne bought of him, and conserves as one of his greatest rarities, in his closet at Whitehall.   This picture I intend to be borrowed of his Majesty, for Mr. Loggan to engrave an accurate piece by, which will sell well both at home and abroad."

whom I intend to see on Monday next, and shall with him sacrifice to your health
in a glasse of sack.   Thus intreating your excuse for this scribled paper, I wish you
all happines, and am, with all my heart, Sir, your most affectionate friend, and most
humble servant, JOHN AUBREY.   *Easton Pierse, Aug.* 30, 1661.   These for his
most honoured friend Mr. Thomas Hobbes, at the Earle of Devonshire's, at Salisbury House in the Strand. Post paid."*

On the 22nd of April, 1663, the Royal Society was incorporated by a charter
granted by King Charles the Second.   Viscount Brouncker was the first President
of the society, and on the Council were, Sir Kenelm Digby, Sir William Petty, and
John Evelyn.   By virtue of a power reposed in them by the charter, the President
and Council, on the 20th of May following, nominated such persons as they thought
desirable as Fellows, and Aubrey was one of those so named: his friends Dryden,
Wren, Hooke,—in fact all the literati of the age,—were also nominated Fellows at
the same time.†   After the first two months new members were elected by vote.
The history of the formation of this society is well known.   There is no doubt that
Aubrey had belonged to it before its incorporation, and perhaps even as early as the
year 1651, when the scientific meetings from which it originated were held in the
chambers of Dr. Petty, and at other places in Oxford.   King Charles II. manifested
considerable interest in the proceedings of the Royal Society, and soon after it was
incorporated he attended the meetings, and held frequent interviews with the
President and many of the most eminent members.   An interesting event in
Aubrey's life had its rise in a conversation of this kind :

" A. D. 1663. King Charles II. discoursing one morning with my Lord Brounker
and Dr. Charlton, concerning Stoneheng, they told his Majestie what they had heard
me say concerning Aubury, for that it did as much excell Stoneheng as a cathedral
does a parish church.   His Majestie admired that none of our chorographers had
taken notice of it, and commanded Dr. Charlton to bring me to him the next
morning.   I brought with me a draught of it, done by memorie only, but well

* This letter was printed many years ago in the *European Magazine*, but I am not aware in whose possession the original then was, nor whether it is still extant.

† Thomson's *History of the Royal Society*, 4to. 1812.

enough resembling it, with which His Majestie was pleased, gave me his hand to kisse, and commanded me to wait on him at Marleborough, when he went to Bath with his Queen (which was about a fortnight after),* which I did ; and the next day, when the court were on their journey, His Majestie left the Queen and diverted to Aubury, with the view whereof he and His Royal Highnesse the Duke of Yorke were very well pleased ; His Majesty then commanded me to write a description of it, and present it to him ; and the Duke of Yorke commanded me to give an account of the old camps and barrows in the plaines. As His Majestie departed from Aubury to overtake the Queen, he cast his eie on Silbury Hill, about a mile off, which he had the curiosity to see, and walkt up to the top of it,† with the Duke of York, Dr. Charlton and I attending them. They went to Lacock to dinner, and that evening to Bathe, all the gentry and commonaltie of those parts waiting on them, with great acclamations of joy, &c. In September following I surveyed that old monument of Aubury with a plane table, and afterwards tooke a review of Stoneheng, and then I composed this following discourse, in obedience to His Majestie's command, and presented it to him, which he commanded me to put in print."‡

In the year 1664 Aubrey went into France. He landed on the 11th of June at Calais, visited Paris, Tours, and Orleans, and returned in October ; beyond which little more is known of his continental tour. There is, however, in the Ashmolean Museum a letter addressed to him by Hobbes whilst he was at Paris, wherein the latter approves of his design of seeing "the Loyer, and the country of Brittany, and that about Geneva ;" and adds, "I see you mean to husband all your time to the best advantage. I have nothing to add but my wishes for your safety and the continuance of yoʳ health, which is not to be despaired of in one that can temper himself from excesses, and especially in fruit, as you can."

* The King commenced this progress on the 26th of August, and returned to London on the 2nd of October. He was sumptuously entertained at Marlborough by Lord Seymour, and at Longleat by Sir James Thynne.

† The following passage in Dr. Stukeley's volume on *Abury* (folio, 1743,) may possibly refer to another visit of the monarch to that interesting temple :—" Some old people remember Charles II., the Duke of York, and Duke of Monmouth *riding* up Silbury Hill." (p. 43)

‡ *Monumenta Britannica*, ut supra.

Aubrey's discovery of the mineral spring at Seend, in Wiltshire, in 1665, has been already noticed. In the same year he says, under the date "Novemb. 1," "I made my first address (in an ill hour) to Joane Sumner."* More than once prior to this, Aubrey had entertained matrimonial projects. In his *Collection of Genitures* (p. 110) he remarks, "My mother fell from her horse, and brake her arme, the last day of April 1649-50, when I was a suitor to Mrs. Jane Codrington." In another paper he says, "About the 16 or 18 April, 1651, I sawe that incomparable good-conditioned gentlewoman, Mrs. M. Wiseman, with whom at first sight I was in love." And he tells us that in 1655 and 1656 he had "several love and lawe suites." And again, "1657. Novemb. 27, obiit Dña Kasker Ryves, with whom I was to marry, to my great losse." But neither Aubrey's connexion with Mrs. Codrington, nor Mrs.† Wiseman, nor even with "Dña Kasker Ryves," through whose untimely death he had so great a loss, were equally unfortunate in their results with that which he now formed with Mrs. Joan Sumner: for in December 1667 he was arrested in Chancery-lane at her suit. In February following he, with some difficulty, obtained a verdict against her, with £600 damages, in a trial at Salisbury; but the amount of those damages was reduced to £300 on a new trial at Winchester in 1669, and in those days, as at present, even that amount was probably insufficient to defray his costs, still less to compensate him for the annoyance and anxiety attendant on such proceedings. Well might he say "*in an ill hour* I made my first address to Joan Sumner." However, it must be borne in mind that we have only the *ex-parte* statements of Aubrey in this matter, and that the lady doubtless considered herself an equal sufferer by it.

It is strange that Dr. Rawlinson, with Aubrey's manuscript before him, in which these circumstances are mentioned, should have inferred from it that he was married. He observes, "He returned from France in October 1664, *when our author was married*, but to whom he has not thought fit to tell; perhaps because he repented of his match, as seems to be implied in a note, where he says that on

---

* *Accidents of John Aubrey*, ante, p. 19.

† Unmarried females were in Aubrey's time called "mistresses," *miss* being in fact a modern abbreviation, introduced probably to contradistinguish them from married women.

Novr 1, 1665, he made his first addresses (in an ill hour) to Joan Sumner:"* and in accordance with this remark of Dr. Rawlinson all authors who have since written memoirs of Aubrey, have repeated the statement that he was unhappily married.

A careful examination of all our antiquary's correspondence and memoranda has however enabled me to give an unqualified contradiction to this statement. It will be shown hereafter that not only was he unmarried eight years after the time to which this note refers, but that he died a bachelor.

* Memoir prefixed to Aubrey's *History of Surrey*.

Chap. III.

ABOUT the year 1667, during one of his visits to Oxford, Aubrey became acquainted with Anthony à Wood, and till within a short time of the latter's death a friendly and familiar intercourse continued to subsist between them. Wood, in his *Diary*, gives a minute account of the commencement of their acquaintance. In quoting this however it is essential to premise, that the contemptuous language it applies to Aubrey, does not convey Wood's opinion of him at the time now referred to, for the article containing it was unquestionably written long afterwards;—probably indeed so late as 1693 or 1694. On any other supposition Wood can only be regarded as acting in a most deceitful manner; for throughout this interval of more than five-and-twenty years, it is known that they maintained a continuous correspondence, conducted on both sides in the warmest and most friendly terms. The passage referred to is as follows: " An. 1667.* John Aubrey of Easton Piers in the parish of Kington St. Michaël, in Wiltsh., was in Oxon. with Edw. Forest a bookseller, living against Alls. coll. to buy books. He then saw lying on the stall *Notitia Academiæ Oxoniensis;*† and asking, who the author of that book was? he [Edw. Forest] answer'd, the report was, that one M^r. Anth. Wood, of Merton coll. was the author, but was not. Whereupon M^r. Aubrey, a pretender to antiquities,

---

* In page 16, ante, it will be seen that Aubrey affixes the date 1665 to the name of Wood, in his list of *Amici*, but this is doubtlessly incorrect.

† Fulman's *Academiæ Oxoniensis Notitia* was published in 1665, 4to.

having been contemporary to A. Wood's elder brother* in Trin. coll. and well acquainted with him, he thought, that he might be as well acquainted with A. W. himself. Whereupon repairing to his lodgings, and telling him who he was,† he got into his acquaintance, talk'd to him about his studies, and offer'd him what assistance he could make, in order to the completion of the work that he was in hand with.‡ Mr. Aubrey was then in a sparkish garb, came to towne with his man and two horses, spent high, and flung out A. W. at all reckings. But his estate of 700*li.* per an. being afterwards sold, and he reserving nothing of it to himself, liv'd afterwards in a very sorry condition, and at length made shift to rub out by hanging on Edm. Wyld, esq., living in Blomesbury neare London, on James earle of Abendon, whose first wife was related to him, and on Sr Joh. Aubrey, his kinsman, living somtimes in Glamorganshire and somtimes at Borstall neare Brill in Bucks. He was a shiftless person, roving and magotieheaded, and somtimes little better than crased. And being exceedingly credulous, would stuff his many letters sent to A. W. with folliries, and misinformations, which somtimes would guid him into the paths of errour."§

Now it is evident from the above extract that it could not have been written at the beginning of the intimacy of Wood and Aubrey; and in a future page some reasons, it is hoped of a conclusive nature, will be offered, tending to show that it was penned about the year 1693. In the meantime it may be sufficient to show that the spirit of it is totally opposed to the feelings with which they regarded each other soon after their acquaintance commenced, by adverting to some letters which passed between them at the beginning of the year 1668. On the 8th of January in that year Aubrey wrote to Wood, probably for the first time, as follows: "Deare Sir, I must never forgett your kindnesse to me when at Oxon. I must assure you I esteeme myselfe very happy in yor acquaintance. As often as I may serve you pray let me heare from you, for I am to my power as zealous for you as any one in

---

* Edward Wood, who was of Trinity College from 1643 till his death in 1655.

† Aubrey's age at this time was 42 ; Wood was about 7 years younger.

‡ Most probably the *History and Antiquities of the University of Oxford*, which however was not published till 1674.

§ Wood's *Auto-biography*, in Bliss's edit. of *Athen. Oxon.*, vol. i. p. lx.

this nation."* In reply to this Wood says, "I wish I had acquaintance with more of y^r publick spirit, who might satisfie me of such matters."† Other letters from Aubrey, written on the 19th of July, and on the 11th of November, in the same year, are couched in similar terms. In the latter he says: "I write in hast (not yet having finished my lawe suite). I will lengthen my life a little, by reviving my spirits at Oxon."‡

Up to this time it is clear, from the account by Anthony à Wood above quoted, that Aubrey enjoyed a handsome income; but we find that he was soon afterwards under the necessity of selling nearly all his property, a result which Wood seems to infer was the consequence of his own extravagance or mismanagement. A " shiftless" im-providence is by no means an inconsistent feature in the character of the generous John Aubrey, but it may be presumed that the failure of law-suits in which, perhaps without any imprudence on his own part, he had become involved, had at least an equal influence in producing this reverse of fortune. Before his father's death he had been summoned home from Oxford "to look after his country business, and solicite a Lawe suite;" § and his father died, "leaving him," as he somewhat obscurely says, " debts 1800 *lib.* and law proceed. 1,000 *lib.*"§ Only four or five years afterwards he " began his chargeable and tedious lawe suite on the Entaile in Brecknockshire and Monmouthshire,"|| which suit he elsewhere says " cost him 1,200 *lib.*"§ In 1655 and 1656 he tells us that he had " several love and lawe suites;"|| and besides these, as already mentioned, he was harassed, at a later period, not only with " treacheries and enmities in abundance," but with legal proceedings respecting Mrs. Sumner. References to the law suit on the entail in Brecknockshire are of frequent occurrence in Aubrey's manuscripts. He mentions Thomas Corbet, Esq. of Gray's Inn, and Judge Rumsey, as his counsel, the latter specially " about the entaile."¶

---

* Original in the *Ballard Coll. of Letters, Bodleian Library*, vol. xiv.
† Copy, in Wood's handwriting, indorsed on the above.
‡ Original in the same volume.
§ *Autobiography, ante.*
|| *Accidents of John Aubrey, ante.*
¶ *Lives of Eminent Men*, vol. ii. p. 359, 522.

One of his notes runs thus:— "I have the Deed of Entaile of the Lands in Brecon. and Monmouth. South Wales, by my great-grandfather William Aubrey, LL.D. wch lands now of right belong to me."* And in his *Life of Dr. Aubrey* he more fully states his claim to the estates in question, as follows:— " He [Dr. A.] purchased Abercunvrig (the ancient seate of the family) of his cosen Aubrey. He built the great house at Brecknock; his studie lookes on the river Uske. He could ride nine miles together in his owne land in Breconshire. In Wales and England he left 2500 *lib.* per ann. whereof there is now none left in the family. . . . . . He made a deed of entaile (36 Eliz.) wch is also mentioned in his will, whereby he entailes the Brecon estate on the issue male of his eldest son, and in defailer, to skip the 2d son (for whom he had well provided, and had married a great fortune) and to come to the third. Edward the eldest had seaven sonnes, his eldest son, Sir Will. had also seaven sonnes, and so I am heere the 18th man in remainder, wch putts me in mind of Dr. Donne,

" For what doth it availe
" To be the twentieth man in an entaile?" †

Entangled in such a net of litigation, it is not surprising that Aubrey was ultimately in fear of his creditors, and apprehensive not only of legal proceedings during his life but of the seizure and destruction of his literary labours after his death.

As early as 1661 and 1662 he sold his two estates in Herefordshire. The manor of Burleton near Hereford, which had belonged to his father, he disposed of to Dr. F. Willis, and an estate, the name of which he writes as Stratford, or Strafford, [meaning perhaps Stretford, a small parish near Leominster,] to Herbert Croft, Bishop of Hereford.‡ Some letters from the reverend prelate respecting this purchase are in Aubrey's collection at Oxford. In one he states that " he has made inquiries respecting it, and is assured that, together with the copyhold, the utmost value is a hundred a year; that scarce any improvement can be made in it by the

---

* MS. slip at the end of Aubrey's *Faber Fortunæ.*

† *Lives of Eminent Men,* vol. ii. p. 215.

‡ Consecrated 21 Jan. 1662, and continued bishop of that see till his death in 1691. He is very highly spoken of by *Browne Willis,* and by *Wood* in *Athenæ Oxonienses.*

greatest industry; and that there is scarce enough wood upon it for necessary uses and fences." He complains that there is "so much arable, and so little meadow and pasture." Upon the whole he thinks that "18 years purchase will be in this country the full value; and this," the bishop adds, "I shall give."*

On the 2nd of October, 1669, Aubrey says in a letter to Anthony à Wood, "I shall be the next weeke at Easton-Pierse, where I should be glad to heare from you by the Bristowe Carrier, in Jesus College Lane, to be left at Michaell's-Kington."†
It was perhaps during this sojourn at Easton that Aubrey made a series of rude drawings of the house and grounds, bearing the date 1669.‡ He was there again on the 28th of April following,§ which is the latest trace of his residence at his native place, for Easton-Pierse was sold, and the farm transferred by its tenant to the new landlord at Lady-day 1671. Aubrey considered the transfer of this pro perty an important, or rather a fatal event. He carefully noted not only the day but the hour when it was effected, and drew a scheme or horoscope for the precise time. This is marked "Eston-Pierse possession," with the following note: "25 March 1671. 1. P.M. possession given by Jonathan Rogers to Mr. Sherwin."‖

To illustrate more clearly this crisis in Aubrey's affairs, the passages bearing upon it in his auto-biographical papers may be here repeated. In the first of them he says, "Sold Easton Pierse and the farme at Broad Chalke. Lost 500*li.*, + 200*li.* goods and timber. Absconded as a banished man. Ubi in monte Dei videbitur. I was in as much affliction as a mortall could bee, and never quiet till all was gone. Submitted my selfe to God's will; wholly cast my selfe on God's providence. . . . . Never quiett, nor anything of happiness till $^{\text{divested of all}}_{\text{all was sold}}$ 1670-1671, at what time Providence raysed me unexpectedly good friends." In the other he has the following words: "1669 and 1670. I sold all my estate in Wilts. From 1670 to this very day (I thank God) I have enjoyed a happy delitescency."

* *Coll. of Letters to Aubrey* in the *Ashmolean Museum,* vol. i.

† Original (dated Broad Chalk) in the *Ballard Coll. of Letters, Bodleian Library,* vol. xiv.

‡ "Designatio de Easton-Piers in Com. Wilts. Per me (heu!) infortunatum Johannem Aubrey, R.S. Socium. Anno Dñi 1669." Original in the *Ashmolean Museum.*

§ Date of *Introduction to North Division of Wiltshire, ante,* p. 34.

‖ *Collection of Genitures,* in the *Ashmolean Museum.*

Now, though Aubrey so emphatically says he was at this period of his life " divested of all," there is still reason to believe that he retained some interest in the Broad Chalk farm till a later date ; for, in a letter to Wood, he mentions the death of his mother, in 1686, and says, " My head has been a fountain of teares, and this is the first letter (except of businesse) that I have writt since my Griefe. I am now involved in a great deale of trouble : and *Chalke must be sold :* but I hope to make some reservation for myselfe. . . . I shall shortly goe to Chalke to see how matters goe there."* Perhaps Aubrey continued to hold the lease of that farm from the Earl of Pembroke, but assigned the remainder of the term to Farmer Good, instead of occupying it himself.

Although his circumstances were thus altered, it is gratifying to find that he retained the friendship and esteem of his intellectual associates, and even secured the patronage of other influential and accomplished men whom he mentions in his notes. His resignation and content of mind evince a philosophic disposition ; and it is especially pleasing to observe with what zeal, after his reverses, he applied himself to the prosecution and completion of the literary works which he had commenced.

He writes thus : " A° 1671 having sold all, and disappointed as aforesaid of moneys I rec^d. I had so strong an impulse to (in good part) finish the Description of Wilts in 2 volumes in fol. that I could not be quiett till I had donne it, and that with danger enough, tanquam canis e Nilo, for feare of Crocodiles (i.) Catch-poles."† Besides this he seems to have arranged, and brought into a somewhat finished shape, the work which had its origin in his account of Avebury, and which, embracing, besides notices of Druidical monuments, various antiquities of a general nature, he designated " *Monumenta Britannica.*" This work bears the date 1671, about which time it appears that he contemplated printing it. Moreover he was still actively engaged in collecting materials to assist his friend Wood, for his *History and Antiquities of Oxford.* The latter wrote to him as follows

* Original in the *Ballard Collection of Letters, Bodleian Library*, vol. xiv.

† *Auto-biography*, ante. By the " *Description of Wilts,*" Aubrey means his collections for *North Wiltshire ;* the other work on the county he properly calls the " *Natural History of Wilts.*"

on the 10th of November, 1671: "I am verie glad y^t y^o have satisfied me in so many things, and cease not to send into divers parts for further information of other men: I speake in my conscience (for I have told other men of it already) y^t I have had and shall have more from y^o as to these things then all people besides w^{t}soever. W^t I have had hitherto besides, hath been for the most part by mine owne industry & purse."*

There is no proof that Aubrey devoted his attention to Astrology before the time of his misfortunes; but at the close of 1671 he applied to the celebrated Henry Coley; who, after making the necessary calculations, furnished him with a series of predictions of the events likely to happen to him on every day in the month of January following. At the end of the next year Coley again drew his horoscope in a most elaborate manner, appending similar predictions for the whole of the year 1673. The very minute and circumstantial nature of these prophecies show clearly that Coley must have enjoyed a high degree of popularity to enable him to promulgate, without fear or hesitation, such absurd documents. To the paper last mentioned he prefixes some remarks on a calculation of Aubrey's nativity by his rival, John Gadbury, some of which are perhaps worth quoting. "By M^r. G's good favour," he begins, "if I may presume, I rather take y^s to be ye true Nativity, for ye Gentleman is a nimble, active person, and one y^t to my knowledge ys curious to inspect all things that are learned or ingenious. Then what can be more significant than ☿ in ☌ of ♀ in ye ascendant in ye dignities of ♀? The Native was never yet marryed (though he is is no enemie to ye female Sex), and what better denotes such an accident then ye position of ♄ in ye 7th in ☍ to ♃ and ☿ in the ascendant: it also gives an Impediment in ye Native's speech, and aptly shews great vexations in Love affairs, wch the Native has experienced to purpose." After more to the same effect, Coley concludes thus: "Therefore let Mr. G. try 'tother touch at it, for this looks no more like Esq. Aũ than an apple is like an oyster." The *Collection of Genitures* in which these papers are placed bears the dates " Londini, May 29, 1674," and " 1677," and it shows that about this period Aubrey must have been busily

---

* Original in a *Coll. of Letters to Aubrey* in the *Ashmolean Museum*, vol. ii.

engaged in ascertaining the precise hours of the births of most of his literary friends, and other public characters, having drawn their horoscopes himself, and inserted them, with astrological remarks, in the volume here referred to.

In 1673 Aubrey was still actively engaged in literary pursuits, and on the 2nd of May in that year " Mr. Ogilby, the Royal Cosmographer," granted him a licence to survey the county of Surrey. This very curious document not only tends to show the public estimation of our antiquary, but is a memorable circumstance of the times. It states that " by virtue of His Majesty's warrant, dated 24th August, 1671, authorizing me to proceed in the actual survey of His Majesty's kingdom of England and dominion of Wales, I have constituted, ordained, and made, and by these presents do constitute, ordain, and make John Aubrey, Esq. my lawful Deputy for the county of Surrey and parts adjacent, willing and requiring in His Majesty's name all justices of the peace, mayors, bailiffs, sheriffs, parsons, vicars, &c. to be aiding and assisting my said deputy or his agents in the said actual survey, and upon his reasonable request to admit him free access to all public registers or other books, whereby the geographical and historical description of His Majesty's said kingdom may be any ways promoted or ascertained."* Under the authority of this appointment Aubrey visited all the principal places in Surrey, and collected information from the parish registers, copies of monumental inscriptions, and other historical, topographical, and traditionary details, which were published after his death, with numerous additions, notes, &c. by Dr. Richard Rawlinson, with the double title of " A Perambulation of the County of Surrey," and " The Natural History and Antiquities of the County of Surrey." Aubrey says at the beginning of the work, " I enter'd upon the Perambulation of the County of *Surrey* July 1, 1673, and left off about the middle of *September* following :" an exceedingly short time, as remarked by Manning and Bray, in their history of the county, for the compilation of a county history. But the printed work was probably the result also, in a great measure, of information

---

* The original document, under the hand and seal of Ogilby, is in Aubrey's MS. *Perambulation of Surrey* (in the *Ashmolean Museum*): likewise a printed copy of the King's warrant, authorizing the former to survey and describe the kingdom. Speaking of this transaction Gough says, " One may venture to pronounce Ogilby's plan little better than that of the modern booksellers,—to raise him a little money." (*British Topography*, vol. ii. p. 262.) Aubrey gives some account of Ogilby in his *Lives of Eminent Men.*

H

procured in other visits, and from private and published sources.   Nearly three years afterwards Aubrey submitted his papers on Surrey to the perusal of his friend Evelyn, who thus wrote to him on the 8th of February, 1675-6 : " Sir, With incredible satisfaction have I perus'd your *Natural History of Surrey*, &c. ; and greatly admire both your Industry in undertaking so profitable a Work, and your Judgment in the several Observations which you have made.   It is so useful a Piece, and so obliging, that I cannot sufficiently applaud it.   Something I would contribute to it, if it were possible ; but your *Spicilegium* is so accurate, that you have left nothing almost for those who come after you."   This letter is printed at the beginning of Aubrey's *Surrey*.   The more recent works of Manning and Bray, and Brayley, show that Evelyn greatly overrated the merits of Aubrey's writings.

In the summer of 1673 he was at Hothfield, in Kent, " the seat of my singular good lord, Nicholas E. of Thanet," where he surveyed the parish church in order to establish a theory as to the variation in the positions of old churches, with reference to the cardinal points of the compass.   The church was dedicated to St. Margaret, and he found, or fancied, its position " answer to the sun-rising on St. Margaret's day, 20th July," whence he infers that churches were formerly so placed that their eastern ends should be directly opposite to that part of the horizon where the sun rose on the day of their patron saints.   He says, " I did make this observation precisely on the day of the vernal equinox, 1673, at sun-setting."*

In the same year a set of queries was printed, to be addressed to persons likely to afford information on the subjects to which they referred, with a view to publishing a new edition of Camden's *Britannia*, a task afterwards executed by Bishop Gibson. On a copy of these queries, preserved amongst Aubrey's manuscripts, he has written the following note : " These queries were considered at several meetings by Christ. Wren, John Hoskyns, R. Hook, J. Ogilby, John Aubrey, Gregory King."†

In this year likewise the third and concluding volume of Dugdale's *Monasticon* was published.   It contained (at p. 136.) an account of Osney Abbey, near Oxford,

---

* *Remaines of Gentilisme* (*Lansdowne MS.* 231, *British Museum*), p. 3.

† This paper is annexed to the *Perambulation of Surrey*, in the *Ashmolean Museum*. It will be observed that neither Gibson nor Tanner appear in this list.

accompanied by an engraving with the following inscriptions : " Prospectus Ruinarum Abbatiæ de Osney, juxta Oxon. W. Hollar fecit ;"* and on a tablet, surmounted by a shield bearing the arms of Aubrey with several quarterings, " Insignes hujusce Fabricæ Ruinas, quas Antiquitatis ergò plurimum suspexit Adolescentulus jamtum Oxoniensi ascriptus, & (quod commodum accidit) paulo antequam Bello Civili funditùs e medio tollerentur, delineandas curavit, Posteris quasi redivivas, L. D. C. Q. Johannes Albericus de Eston-Pierse in agro Wilts, Arm."*

The plate is engraved in Hollar's usual style, and there can be no doubt was executed from one of the drawings by Mr. Hesketh, as already mentioned by Aubrey in his Auto-biography (ante, p. 14). Impressions of the same plate were given in the *second* volume of the next edition of the Monasticon† (1682, p. 136), but it was not re-engraved for the new work edited by Caley, &c. In the article *Aubrey*, in the *Biographia Britannica*, this plate is particularly mentioned with approval, and the writer adds " he will certainly be no loser by it who will be at the expense of having it engraved again." Acting perhaps on this hint, Mr. Skelton published a copy of it in his *Oxonia Antiqua Restaurata* (pl. 115). This is not, how-ever, an exact fac-simile of Hollar's plate, either in style or effect, and it wants the original arms and inscriptions.

Besides referring to this print Dr. Rawlinson says that " when that great work the *Monasticon* was in embrio," Mr. Aubrey gave to it " his best assistance." ‡ He was on intimate terms with Sir William Dugdale, but we have no other evidence that he contributed any literary materials to the *Monasticon*.

A work, however, which was deeply indebted for its usefulness to Aubrey's in-dustry, was published in 1674 ; namely, Wood's *Historia et Antiquitates Universitatis*

* " View of the ruins of the abbey of Osney, near Oxford." " The noble ruins of this fabrick, drawn from a love to antiquity, while yet a youth at Oxford, and (which was not a little lucky) but a short time before they were entirely destroyed in the Civil War, secured now, and as it were revived, are dedicated to posterity, by John Aubrey, of Easton Piers, in the county of Wilts, Esq."—Translation of the original Latin, in *Biographia Britannica*, but not rendered with precision.

† Dr. Rawlinson states that " most of the copies of the Monasticon, by some misfortune or other, want this plate." The British Museum copies of both editions, however, have it.

‡ *Life*, prefixed to Aubrey's *Hist. of Surrey*.

Oxoniensis. We have seen how gratefully Wood acknowledged these obligations in a private communication to his friend, and he now publicly thanked him as follows: " Transmissum autem nobis est illud epitaphium a viro per-humano, Johanne Alberico, vulgo Aubrey, armigero, hujus collegii olim generoso commensali, jam vero è Regiâ Societate Londini; viro inquam, tam bono, tam benigno, ut publico solum commodo, nec sibi omnino, natus esse videatur." (lib. ii. p. 297.) This work was originally published in Latin, at the express desire of Bishop Fell (the Dean of Christ Church), who defrayed the expenses of printing it. Wood wished it to be published in English, and felt much annoyed that his wishes on that point were overruled by the Dean; and more especially at some alterations and interpolations which the latter made in the text. Indeed it seems to have been generally thought that the work was injured by appearing first in Latin; and with that feeling the Rev. J. Gutch, M.A., published an edition of it in English, in 3 vols. 4to. 1786-94. Respecting the original Aubrey wrote to Wood before its publication, as follows: " If you wish to have records at Rome searched it shall be done for you; for when I was at Paris I was acquainted with some of the . . . who will undertake it: but one of them this day told me that he does not approve of the Universityes designe in printing it first in Latin, for if it is first in English it will bring it into far more fame and sell the better."*

It is painful to turn again from the relation of these congenial and pleasing occupations, to Aubrey's pecuniary embarassments. Some remarkable letters addressed to him by the Earl of Thanet shew that these still pressed heavily upon him, and at the same time they afford a curious illustration of the customs of the age.

On the 19th of April, 1675, the Earl acknowledges a letter from Aubrey, stating that his friend and patron, Mr. Wyld, was disposed to purchase land in New York. The Earl strongly dissuades him from doing so, and points out how much preferable as an investment a similar purchase would be in the Bermudas; where his lordship himself had an estate.† He then goes on to say, " I am glad you have so good an

---

* *Original*, Feb. 17, 1669, in the *Ballard Collection of Letters, Bodl. Library*, vol. xiv.

† The Earl had previously (30 Nov. 1674) intimated to Aubrey that he was in want of some person to go to Bermuda for him, to attend his land.

opportunity to make your addresses to that excellent lady the younger Countess Dowager of Pembroke; who, if your stars be favourable, may, thro' the interest of the Duchess of Portsmouth, procure y° some good employment, if not neglected by a wonted trapishness incident in you. This freedom I take in mentioning that you will I hope easily forgive, since I do it not by way of check, but by a friendly advertisement to beware of it;" and he concludes with this singular sentence:— "If you have the same occasions of a protection against your merciless creditors as you had some while since, I may now serve y° in it, both with *salvo honore et conscientia*, providing y° will be a little ruled."*

The Earl of Thanet's next letter to Aubrey is of remarkable import—"Hothfield, May 3, 1675. J. Aubrey:—With this y° will receive a protection according to your desire, wch when useless returne. I send it y° under this provisoe, that yow are my Sollicitor to looke after my business in London; and for your Sallary that is agreed on. My mother hath lent me Thanet house garden, where I intend to fit up two or three chambers for my use when I come to London privately, and intend to stay not long there, one of wch as my meniall servant you may make use of when fitted up, and when it is you shall have notice. . . . . . I would have you in the future to take more time in writing your letters, for your last was soe ill writ that I had a great deal of trouble to read some part of it. THANET."† In a short letter written the day afterwards the Earl addresses Aubrey thus:—"Sir, I am well aware the stile of my letter of the 3rd. instant is unfitting to a person of your birth. The reason I made myself such a proud ill-bred fellow in it is the better to disguise the business you lately enjoined me to do for you." He then says that his future letters will be equally cool and distant in their language, so that, if they should ever be subjected to examination, any person would believe "that the business, although very unbefitting, of your belonging to me, is no otherwise than real;" and he adds: "it is the first protection I ever gave." This letter he signs "Your most affectionate and humble servant, THANET."†

Poor Aubrey's troubles appear to have reached their climax about two years

* Original in a *Collection of Letters to Aubrey*, in the *Ashmolean Museum*, vol. ii.
† Ibid.

after this : " July 31, 1677, I *sold my bookes* to Mr. Littlebery; scilicet, when my Impostume in my head did break."* Perhaps to this unfortunate period of his life may be ascribed a loan he obtained from Dr. Edward Davenant. " He was my singular good friend," says Aubrey, " and to whom I have been more beholding then to any one beside ; for I borrowed five hundred pounds of him for a yeare and a halfe, and I could not fasten any interest on him."†

In December, 1679, Thomas Hobbes died. The continuance of his friendship with Aubrey until his death is proved by a letter which he wrote to him only four months previous.‡ Aubrey had been desired by Hobbes to write his life, for the information of posterity, and he accordingly at once set about the task. James Wheldon, the amanuensis and executor of the deceased, wrote to Aubrey narrating the circumstances of his death and funeral, enclosing a copy of his Will, his epitaph on himself, and a " catalogue of his bookes."§

Aided by the information thus derived from Wheldon, Aubrey wrote his *Life of Mr. Thomas Hobbes, of Malmesburie*, but instead of publishing it himself he appears to have lent the manuscript to Dr. Richard Blackbourne, of Trinity College, Cambridge, who in 1681 produced a Latin Life of Hobbes,‖ with which was reprinted the Memoirs (in Latin, Prose and Verse,) previously published, and both supposed to have been written by Hobbes himself. In a list of the friends and associates of the deceased, Dr. Blackbourne thus mentions Aubrey : " Jo. Albericus, vulgo Aubrey, é Soc. Reg. Armig. Amicus ejus in primis, ex Vicinia Malmsburiensi Oriundus, & sub communi Præceptore Institutus, Vir Publico Bono

---

* *Collection of Genitures*, p. 175.

† *Lives of Eminent Men*, vol. ii. p. 300.

‡ Original in the *Ashmolean Museum*, [annexed to Aubrey's *MS. Life of Hobbes*] dated " Chatsworth, Aug. 18, 1679." This letter expresses the writer's regret that " his book of the Civil War has come abroad." It ends as follows : " I pray you present my humble thankes to Mr. Sam. Butler. The privilege of stationers is, in my opinion, a very great hinderance to the advancement of all humane learning. I am, Sir, your very humble servant, Th. Hobbes."

§ The originals of these letters are also annexed to Aubrey's *MS. Life of Hobbes*. The first (which is dated " Hardwick, January the 16th, 1679–80") together with Hobbes's Will, has been printed in *Letters from the Bodleian*, vol. ii. p. 632. The second is dated " Chatsworth, Sept. 7, 1680."

‖ *Thomæ Hobbes Angli Malmesburiensis Philosophi Vita*, 8vo. 1681, pp. 243. A second edition was published in 1682, 4to., pp. 67.

magis quam suo Natus ; qui Princeps mihi scribendi Ansam præbuit, & Materiam humaniter suppeditavit."* According to the custom of the times several *verses*, in commendation of Hobbes, are prefixed to this memoir. They comprise some lines (in English) by Cowley, and others (in Latin) by Dr. Ralph Bathurst, of Trinity College, Oxford, and the following by Aubrey :

> " In Tho. Hobbes.
> Futilis exornet Barbatos pompa Magistros,
> Et Schola Discipulos cogat inepta leves :
> Affulsit nova Lux tenebroso Hobbesius Orbi,
> Quanta est Laus Hominem restituisse sibi ?
>
> Jo. Awbrey, Arm. è Soc. Reg."†

In 1680 Aubrey addressed his *Lives of Eminent Men* to Anthony à Wood, in a letter which is printed with the *Lives* (vol. ii. p. 197). This, he expressly states, was a work he never thought of undertaking had not the latter imposed it upon him, evidently with a view to his *Athenæ Oxonienses*, which was then in progress ; and the following unpublished note gives additional proof of the author's object in collecting these curious biographical details : "My will and humble desire is that these minutes, which I have hastily and scriblingly here set down, be delivered carefully to my deare honored friend, Mr. Anthony à Wood, antiquary of Oxford. Jo. Aubrey. Ascension day, 1680."‡ This manuscript was soon afterwards mentioned in the following strange terms by Wood : "Mr. Aubrey, I beseech yº as yº have been civill in giving this book to me at Oxon in Sep.

---

* "John Aubrey of the Royal Society, Esqʳ ; one of his oldest Friends, born in the neighbourhood of Malmesbury ; educated under the same master. A man born rather for the public good than his own, who chiefly encouraged me to the undertaking this work, and kindly supplied me with materials." *Translation* in *Biographia Britannica.*

† " *On Thomas Hobbes.*
Exterior gravity may Schools erect,
Where Idle Folks may empty Notions scan ;
But Hobbes new light did on the World reflect,
How great his Praise who MAN made known to MAN ?
Jo. AWBREY, Esq. of the Royal Society." *Translation* in *Biographia Britannica.*

‡ Original on the first leaf of the manuscript of the *Lives*, part i.

1681, so I hope w^n y^o have done with it you'l returne every part of it againe to yor serv^t Ant. Wood.   11 Novr 1681."*

Thus it appears that the work was absolutely transferred by Aubrey to Wood; but it seems to have been at different times in the possession of each of them, the author continuing to make additions to it.   He survived Wood, and it was ultimately deposited with his other papers in the Ashmolean Museum.

In 1683 we find Aubrey using great exertions to induce either the University of Oxford, or Trinity College, to purchase the mathematical library of his late friend Sir Jonas Moore.   There are letters to him on this subject from Dr. Wallis and Sir Isaac Newton.   The latter informs him that the college was unable to buy them on account of the heavy charge it had incurred for the new buildings, but that he had acquainted the Vice-Chancellor with the opportunity that offered, though he knew not whether the university would purchase, " their chest being at present very low."†

One of Aubrey's most curious and least-known manuscripts, bearing the date "168$\frac{3}{4}$," is called *An Idea of Education of Young Gentlemen*, being an elaborate plan for a more popular and useful system of education than that which was adopted in his time, or is, even in the present day, carried out at the Universities. It " had its conception," he says, as early as 1669; and, in forwarding the manuscript to Mr. Anthony Henley, of the Grange, in Hampshire, he expresses a great desire to have it put in practice.‡   To Anthony à Wood likewise, speaking of his manuscripts, he says, " That I most value is my *Idea of Education of Young Gentlemen*," and he evinces much anxiety as to its fate after his decease.§

Soon after its completion this " Idea" was perused by the Rev. Andrew Paschal, of Chedzoy, in Somersetshire, who, in a letter to the author, expressed a very high opinion of it.||

* Original in the manuscript of the *Lives*, part iii.

† Original, dated " Oxford, Decr 23, 1683," in a *Collection of Letters to Aubrey*, in the *Ashmolean Museum*, vol. ii.

‡ *Letter* annexed to the Original manuscript in the *Ashmolean Museum*.

§ Original in the *Ballard Collection of Letters, Bodleian Library*, vol. xiv.

|| Aubrey's *Surrey*, vol. i. p. xiv.   The *Original* is in a *Collection of Letters to Aubrey* in the *Ashmolean Museum*, vol. ii.

Aubrey's name is mentioned in a letter of about this time with reference to the library of Ralph Sheldon, Esq. of Bewley, Worcestershire, and of Weston, Warwickshire, a great collector and liberal patron of antiquarian literature. Anthony à Wood frequently visited that gentleman, and made a catalogue of his books and papers. Sheldon was likewise a friend to Aubrey, who had access to his library for literary purposes. He died in July, 1684, and by his Will bequeathed £40 to Wood, requesting him to see "his Pedigrees, and all his MSS., and other papers, (except such as were written with his owne hand-writing,) delivered into the Heralds' Office."* At this time Sir William Dugdale was Garter King-at-Arms, and John Dugdale, his son, was Windsor Herald. They entertained a natural desire to procure for the Heralds' Office, under the above bequest, as many of Sheldon's books as possible; and Aubrey, who was then living in London, participated in the desire. On the 22nd of July he wrote to Elias Ashmole thus: "I presume Ant. Wood will do his best with Mr. Sheldon's heir to get his bookes for the Heralds' Office."†

John Dugdale however had occasion, on the 16th of December following, to address his father (who was absent in Warwickshire) as follows: "Mr. Aubray this day told me (wth trouble of mind) that Mr Parker, comīng to the Executor of Mr Sheldon, when the Books were all in hampers, and being told w^t they were, desired to see the Catalogue; whereupon he caused all the Books to be taken out, and advised the Executor to detaine all such Manuscripts as did not relate to Herauldrie: wch he did accordingly; and how to get them will be hard to contrive, I doubt."‡ After this some angry letters passed between Wood and Sir William Dugdale, on the subject of this supposed detention of a part of the books and papers, the latter suspecting that Wood was in some degree a party to it; and Wood in one of his letters assumed that Sir William had been "misinformed by some envious Coxcombe."§

---

* Original in the Prerogative Office, Doctors' Commons. (See Hamper's *Life of Sir W. Dugdale*, p. 138, 434.)

† Copy indorsed by Aubrey on a letter from the Rev. Andrew Paschal. *Collection of Letters to Aubrey, ut supra*, vol. ii.

‡ Hamper's *Life of Sir W. Dugdale*, p. 442.

§ *Ibid.* p. 455. One of the most curious and valuable of the books said to have been detained is now in the Bodleian Library. It is described in the catalogue of MSS. relating to England as, " An ancient and very fair Leiger Book of Glasstenbury Abbey, usually called *Secretum Abbatis*, being alwaies in his own custody." Aubrey, who frequently quotes it in his *North Division of Wiltshire*, calls it *Secretum Domini*.

Sir James Long, of Draycot, Baronet, in a letter to Aubrey* about this time, promised to send him "some cloth for a winter suit," and "four cheeses" made on his own land, which he hoped would prove of good quality. It has been asserted that Aubrey was dependent on the family of Sir James Long, but it must be observed that no such inference should be drawn from this letter, for both the cloth and the cheese were products for which North Wiltshire was even then famous, and therefore such articles were peculiarly appropriate as friendly presents, without necessarily implying poverty on the part of the recipient.

Aubrey witnessed the coronation procession of James II. in 1685, an event which must have called up reminiscences of his interview with the new sovereign, twenty years before, at Avebury. His only record of the ceremony, however, refers to an occurrence, afterwards looked upon as ominous, and as such mentioned in his *Miscellanies*:—"The canopy (of cloth of gold), carried over the king's head by the Wardens of the Cinque Ports was torn by a puff of wind, as he came to Westminster Hall: it hung down very lamentably; I saw it."

At this time Aubrey made numerous additions to his work upon the *Natural History of Wiltshire*. He wrote a title-page and preface to it, both of which bear the date "London, Gresham Coll.: June 6, 1685;" and he now made the fair copy, which is preserved in the library of the Royal Society: the original manuscript being at Oxford. It is not improbable that he expected and hoped the Royal Society would print the work; and it was perhaps with this view that he inscribed it to the Earl of Pembroke, President of the society. Long previously (as he wrote to Wood) their Secretary, hearing of the manuscript, thought fit that the society should be made acquainted with it, and, as Aubrey further states, the inspection of it " gave them two or three dayes entertainment, wch they were pleased to like."†

In 1686 (Feb. 2) he says that "William Penn, Lord Proprietor of Pennsylvania, did give him a grant under his seale of 600 acres in Pennsylvania without his seeking or dreaming of it ;"‡ and he also had a gift of a thousand acres of land in

---

* Original in *Collection of Letters to Aubrey, ut supra*, vol. i.
† Original, dated " Twelfe day, 1675," in the *Ballard Collection, ut supra*.
‡ *Faber Fortunæ*, in the *Ashmolean Museum*.

the island of Tobago, from Captain Poyntz ;* but these lands were doubtless una-
vailable for useful purposes.   At an earlier period of his life, when in greater
pecuniary difficulties, he seems to have contemplated emigration.†

The following letter to Wood is interesting.   "London. May 11, 1686.   Deare
Friend; In January last after a very great conflict of affliction I rowsed up my spts.
and writt a lr̃e to you, and immediately fell to worke with my *Naturall History of
Wilts*, wch I had just donne April 21, (*i.*) rough hewn, and finished the last chapter,
when at ye evening I heard of ye sad news of ye Decease of my deare & ever hon^d
mother: who died at Chalke, but my bro: has buried her with my father in North
Wilts (Kington St. Mich:).   My head has been a fountain of teares, & this is the
first lr̃e (except of businesse) that I have writt since my Griefe.   I am now involved
in a great deale of trouble: & Chalke must be sold: but I hope to make some reservation for myselfe: and I hope before I dye to be able to make an honorable present
to you: for I am for ye Spaniards way; *sc.* not to make my soule my Executor.   I
shall shortly goe to Chalke to see how matters goe there: and as soon as I can pick
up a little money intend to see you at Oxon, and thinke the time very long till I am
wth you.   Sir W. Dugdale's Paules is to be reprinted at Oxon: there is a mistake in
D^r A's. Insc. *sc.* Atavus for Proavus.   Mr. Ashmole & wife is angry wth him for
making such a scandalous Will.   I shall bring severall mãms wth me to insert.
God blesse you & comfort me, y^t I may but live to finish & publish my papers.

"Tuissimus, J. A.

"my true love to Kit Wase, of whõ ye E. of Pembroke & I had much discourse at
dinner, with much respect.   ☞ Let me desire you to write to me by the next
post, to let me know how you doe: yor letter will be a Cordial to me: therefore
pray fail not.   Fab. Philips is yo^rs.   I am sorry for the losse of our facetious friend
Parson Hodges.   I must make hast wth my papers, for I am now 60."‡

* *Faber Fortunæ*, in the *Ashmolean Museum.*

† "1676. From Sir W. Petty. 500 lib. gives in Jamaica 100 lib. p ann.   Take a Chymist with me, for
Brandy, Sugar, &c. and goe half with him." *Ibid.*   And, in a letter to Wood, dated 1674, "I have been very
busy lately (and chiefly with my Lord Vaughan) newly made governor of Jamaica, who is like to spirit me
along with him thither, and has promised me to looke out some place suitable to the qualitie of a gentleman.
The Earl of Thanet would have me goe to his Estate in the Bermudas." Original in the *Ballard Collection,*
ut supra.

‡ Original in the *Ballard Collection, ut supra.*

Chap. IV.

I HAVE now to notice a curious paper, which not only shows the high value Aubrey set upon his Wiltshire Collections, but also, in conjunction with other passages in his writings, that he entertained a constant fear of sudden death while travelling. This is a document in the shape of a *Will*, but it has reference only to his Wiltshire papers:

WILL.

"WHE'AS I JOHN AUBREY R.S.S. doe intend shortly to take a journey into the West: and reflecting on yᵉ Fate that Manuscripts use to have after the death of the author, I have thought good to signify my Last Will (as to this Naturall History of Wilts) that my Will and desire is, that in case I shall depart this life before my returne to London again, to finish, if it pleaseth GOD, this Discourse; I say, and declare, that my Will then is, that I bequeath these papers of yᵉ Naturall History of Wilts to my worthy friend Mʳ Robert Hooke of Gresham Colledge & R.S.S., and I doe also humbly desire him, & my Will is, that the noble Buildings and Prospects should be engraven by my worthy friend Mr. David Loggan, who hath drawn my Picture already in order to it. Witnesse hereunto my hand & seale the eighteenth day of August Año Domini One thousand six hundred eighty and six.

"JO: AUBREY.

"Signed

" Signed and Sealed in the presence
of us

" Fransis Lodwik
  Jo. Godfrey, sen.
  Sam^{ll}. Meverell
  Henry Spencer.

* But two or three sheetes.

"Mďm. there are deposited in the hands of my honoured friend Elias Ashmole, Esq. two Manuscripts of my Writing, viz : Templa Druidum & Chronologia Antiquaria: being both about 3 quires of paper : which doe belong to this Historie & to be printed with it. My Chronologia Architectonica* is at the beginning of the first part of my Antiquities of Wilts; wch are deposited in the hands of my worthy friend Mr Anthony à Wood of Merton College in Oxford: & they will deliver the afor-sayd Manuscripts to ye sayd Mr Robert Hooke."†

In 1687 and 1688 Aubrey wrote his *Remaines of Gentilisme and Judaism,* now in the British Museum,‡ dedicating it to Edmund Wyld, Esq. in the former year. It consists of extracts from the Greek and Roman writers, with illustrations tending to prove that most of the old provincial customs and observances in England were derived from those of the ancients.

About this time Aubrey came to the determination of depositing his manuscripts in the museum at Oxford. That building had been erected by the University, from Sir Christopher Wren's designs, in 1682; and in the next year the collection of curiosities, previously belonging to the Tradescants of Lambeth, was placed in it by Elias Ashmole, to whom John Tradescant, the son, had given them. The museum was in fact built upon the understanding that the Ashmole collection would be deposited there on its completion, and it has ever since borne the name of *The Ashmolean Museum.* Considering Aubrey's anxiety for the preservation of his literary papers, it is evident that he would need very little persuasion by Ashmole to avail himself of this eligible mode of effecting his object. That his friend felt equally anxious they should accompany his collection is shown by the following letter, ad-

† From the Original MS. in my possession. It appears to have been a leaf of the *Natural Hist. of Wilts.*
‡ *Lansdowne MS.* No. 231, (*British Museum*).

dressed to Anthony à Wood:—" London, 22 Dec. 1688. Mr. Wood, Last Tuesday I went to see Mr. Ashmole, whom I found ill. He lately received a letter from Dr Plot,* about the things that I sent to Oxford; and says that he desired you to send to the Museum, but you denied it, and would not let him see the Catalogue that I sent. Mr Ashmole desired to speake with me about it, & is most outrageously angry; & charg'd me to write to y° as soon as I could, to put the box in the Museum: for he looks upon you as a P.,† and saith so does the whole Universitie. . . . . Mr. Ashmole says that now there is such care & good method taken, that the Books in the Museum are more safe than those in the Library or Archives; and he says he expects to heare of your being plunder'd, & papers burnt, as at the Spanish Ambassador's, at *Wild house,* where were burnt MSS. & antiquities invaluable, such as are not left in ye world. . . . . Since therefore it is so order'd, I do desire & appoint y° to send my box forthwith (y° may keep ye key), for feare that all my MSS. &c. should be rifled by y^e *mobile,* (which God forbid, but Mr E. Ashmole & I doe much feare it,) besides my gift will make a better shew in ye Museum than when dispersed in two places. . . . . I have several other MSS. of my own and Mr Mercator's. That of mine that I most value is my Idea of Education of Young Gentlemen, which is in a box as big as that sent to you; with choice Gramaticall bookes both ancient & modern for ye Informations to peruse and study. If I should die here they will be lost or seized upon by Mr Kent's son :‡ if I send them to the Museum the tutors would burn it, for it crosses their interest exceedingly: if in your hands when y° die your nephew will stop guns with them. I intended ye E. of Abingdon, but he has now other fish to fry. I think ye E. of Pembroke would do best, but had I money to pay an amanuensis, I would leave a copy in the hands of each of those two peers.   " Tuissimus, J. AUBREY."§

* The doctor was the first keeper of the Museum.

† Meaning a *Papist.* This letter was written at the time of the Revolution, a circumstance which explains this and other allusions in it.

‡ A subsequent letter, " 16 January, 1689-90," gives us another proof that Aubrey's pecuniary affairs were still unsettled: " I have been extremely busy, & I much feare the next term I shall be engaged in more trouble. I waived a Chancery suite two terms when I was at Oxford, which was the reason I stayed there so long." *Collection of Letters to Aubrey, ut supra,* vol. i.

§ Original in a *Collection of Letters to Aubrey, ut supra,* vol. i.

Very soon after this was written the majority of Aubrey's gifts to the Museum were probably placed there, and a rough catalogue made of them; for the following contemporary entry appears in a manuscript *Register of the Benefactors to the Museum*: "M.D. 1689. Johannes Aubrey, de Easton Piers apud Wiltonienses, Arm. è Soc. Reg. Socius, olim Alumnus, præter Libellos, tum MSS. tum impressos, plus minus Octaginta, diversas illustrium virorum Effigies, Numismata Romana, Eorumq, matrices lateritias, Operis item Musivi sive Tesselati specimen."

In 1690 Aubrey again wrote to Wood: "Upon the receipt of yours I will by the next waggon send down a box full of manuscripts & printed books. The noble E. of Pembroke gave me not long since as many good books as cost him I believe *5li.* Thus hoping to hear from y° I rest in hast, Yours, J. Aubrey. In my next I shall send you three or four obits. I wish heartily my papers were in your hands, for death seems to threaten.—God blesse you & me in this in-&-out-world."*

In the same year (the *Athenæ* and *Fasti Oxonienses* being then on the eve of publication,) Aubrey made some further collections in biography, as intimated by a few sheets of manuscript with that date, entitled, *An Apparatus for the Lives of our English Mathematical Writers.*†

At the beginning of 1692 he commenced a correspondence with Dr. James Garden, Professor of Divinity in King's College, Aberdeen, upon the subject of Celtic monuments, and Scottish customs and traditions. The learned doctor furnished Aubrey with much valuable information respecting the stone circles of North Britain, the Orkney islands, &c., which they both concurred in regarding as sacred temples of the Druids. This correspondence continued about three years, and, besides the subjects mentioned, Dr. Garden's letters comprise disquisitions on the less important themes of "Second-sight," "Transportation by an invisible power," and other superstitions of the age. Aubrey applied this information to his *Remaines of Gentilisme*, and *Monumenta Britannica;* and his correspondent's letters (most of which are still preserved in the Ashmolean Museum), are referred to with commendation by Bishop Gibson, in his edition of Camden's *Britannia*, as well as, in

* Original, dated "10 May, 1690," in the *Ballard Collection, ut supra.*
† Original in the *Ashmolean Museum.*

later times, by Gough and other writers. Two of them are printed in Aubrey'
Miscellanies, (though without the name of their author), and one is also published
in the first volume of *Archæologia,* p. 312.

At the persuasion of Anthony à Wood Aubrey revised and transcribed his
Perambulation, or *History of Surrey,* making some additions to it with reference to
Southwark; and the dates "St. Thomas-day, 1691," and "May 1, 1692,"* fix the
time when he did so. Still, though always contemplating it, a reluctance to print
anything which could be regarded as incomplete or imperfect seems to have
restrained him from publishing either the Surrey or the Wiltshire collections, or any
of his other works, some of which were by this time very minute and copious. He
however lent them to his friends for perusal and correction. Thus, on the 15th of
September, 1691, he forwarded his *Natural History of Wilts* to John Ray, the
botanist and zoologist, who returned it on the 27th October following, and who, in
acknowledging its receipt, as well as in sending it back to Aubrey, spoke in the
most favourable terms of the work, suggesting some trifling improvements, and
strongly urging him to "speed it to the Presse."† Aubrey visited Ray, at Black
Notley, in the summer of 1692, and perhaps then left with him another manuscript,
respecting which the latter wrote to him soon afterwards as follows: "Your
Adversaria Physica I have read over once, but the variety and curiosity of the matter
and observations is such that I cannot satisfy myself with a single reading."‡
To "his ever honoured Friend, John Evelyn," Aubrey, at this time, sent his favorite
Idea of Education, saying, "In case I should happen to die before I call for this Idea,
I desire you then to leave it with Dr Hooke at Gresham College, to be putt into my
Chest marked Idea: wch is full of Books for this Designe."§ Thus we see that he
was still unwilling to send this work to Oxford, where it has nevertheless been safely

* See *Address to the Reader,* and commencement of the printed work.
† Original Letters in the *Ashmolean Museum.* They are printed entire in Aubrey's *Lives of Eminent
Men,* vol. ii. p. 158, and Aubrey's *Surrey,* vol. v. p. 408.
‡ Letter, printed in *Lives of Eminent Men,* vol. ii. p. 162. Original (24 August, 1692,) in the
Ashmolean Museum. Other letters from Ray to Aubrey in the same collection show that the former had
also read the *Perambulation of Surrey,* and the *Idea of Education.*
§ Letter appended to the original MS. in the *Ashmolean Museum* (dated "May 10th, 1692").

kept ever since his death. The new keeper of the Ashmolean Museum, Edward Llhwyd, informed Aubrey (March 1692-3) that he had made a catalogue of his books in that museum, and was engaged in making another of his manuscripts. He further says, " I have got all your pamphlets in yᵉ museum bound, and in case you are disposed to dedicate your *Collection of Letters* to yᵉ museum, I will take care to have them bound out of hand : unlesse yᵒ have been at that charge already yourselfe."* Perhaps we are indebted to Llhwyd's influence with Aubrey for the preservation of the interesting *Collection of Letters* to him, so often quoted. The series, now in the Ashmolean Museum, comprises nearly four hundred letters, alphabetically arranged, and bound in two volumes.

The important light in which Aubrey viewed his papers at this period of his life is further illustrated by his correspondence with the celebrated Dr. Thomas Tanner, (afterwards bishop of St. Asaph). In July 1692, and December 1693, Dr. Tanner had in his possession, besides others of Aubrey's papers, his manuscript work on the Antiquities of *North Wiltshire*, of which, as well as of the *Monumenta Britannica*, and *Remaines of Gentilisme*, he appears to have thought very favourably, and to have been anxious for their publication or preservation. Aubrey also sent him, at his urgent request, the *Natural History of Wiltshire*, in February 1694. These circumstances are detailed in three interesting epistles, which are printed in *Letters from the Bodleian*, (vol. ii. p. 164,) and in another, of earlier date, prefixed by Aubrey to his *Monumenta Britannica*. In the latter Tanner thus writes : " I shall go toward Lavington on Saturday next. My principal business is to drive on our common design, viz. the *Antiquities of Wilts*, which I hope will find encouragement. If it does not I will never undertake anything more for the public. My Sᵗ *Cuthbert's Life* hath suffered the fate of a great many better books. I am heartily sorry your *Monumenta* meets with no better encouragement in this age, but I like it never the worse for that.† It hath been the ill fortune of the best books that they have

---

* Original, in a *Collection of Letters to Aubrey* in the *Ashmolean Museum*, vol. i.

† Aubrey had made some efforts for the publication of this work without success. Writing to Wood in 1687 he said : " As soon as the Terme ends I will perform my Promise to Sʳ W. Dugdale, viz. to make fitt for the Presse my *Templa Druidum*." This was the first chapter of the *Monumenta Britannica*. Wood

K

not borne the charges of their own impression. It is well known that no bookseller would give Sir Henry Spelman five pounds in books for his incomparable *Glossary*, and you know that Sr Walter Raleigh burnt the latter part of his admirable *History of the World*, because the former had undone the printer. The *X Scriptores* and the *Monasticon*, volumes now worth old gold, had never been printed had not the former been carried on by a public fund, the other by the sole charges of the Editor. I hope to live to see the *Monumenta Britannica* in as good vogue as the best of them."*

In another of these letters is the following passage : " I was heartily sorry to hear of your affliction by that tormenting disease the gout ; but was more troubled at that you told me at the bottom of your letter, viz. that you were so far stricken in years. I have seen, heard and read of the notorious misfortunes that usually attend posthumous papers, so that I hope you will make haste, and yourself communicate the greatest and best part of your labourious collections to the world. Your entire originalls shall be deposited hereafter in the Musæum according to your desire, that posterity may see how just we have been to the memory of your pains."

In the month of August, 1692, Aubrey thus wrote to Anthony à Wood : " Accidentally I spoke with Mr Gadbury, who is extremely incenst against you. He tells me what you have wrote, and I am sorry for it, for he was civil to you, and was an ingeniose loyall person. He sayes that you have printed lyes concerning him, and he wonders you should meddle with him, having never been of the University."†
The complaint by Gadbury, here mentioned, probably applied to a brief sketch of his life, incidentally given by Wood in the *Athenæ Oxonienses*, in which he states

urged him to print the *Templa Druidum*, "by itselfe rather than in another book, for if in another ye author of y^t book will carry away ye credit ;" and Tanner, with reference to his design of printing the *first part* of the *Monumenta* only, advised him that it would be " more to his interest, and quite as honorable" for him, "to abridge it *all*, and print it in about 40 sheets ; which would make a very fair 8vo or 4to :" but unfortunately these recommendations were never acted upon. Besides by Wood and Tanner, the *Monumenta* is highly spoken of, in letters to the author, from Gibson, Bathurst, Llhwyd, Charlet and others.

* This lamentable account of the state of authorship and publication is too much paralleled in our own times, and in the history of the " Wiltshire Topographical Society." Bishop Tanner and Aubrey earnestly sought for patronage and support to produce topographical elucidations of their native county. Mr. P. Wyndham, Sir Richard C. Hoare, and the author of the present volume, have laboured hard and zealously in the same cause, and with scarcely better success.

† Original, 20th August, 1692, in the *Ballard Collection, ut supra.*

that the former, after having been apprenticed to a tailor at Oxford, improved "his natural genius for the making of almanacs," under William Lilly, and "set up the trade of almanac-making and fortune-telling for himself; in which he became eminent."* This appears to have been true; and it was certainly much less offensive than the terms in which Lilly speaks of "that monster of ingratitude, my quondam taylor, John Gadbury."† In replying to the above letter Wood expresses much surprise that Gadbury should have felt annoyed at his remarks; and says, "Pray recommend me to him, and desire him, y^t if I speake any things y^t are untrue, he may rectifie them; put them into y^r hands, and to be sent to me."‡

Thus far ample proof has been adduced of the continuance of a cordial friendship between Wood and Aubrey; but, almost simultaneously with the letter last quoted, Aubrey wrote upon the manuscript of the second part of his *Lives of Eminent Men* as follows :

"INGRATITUDE.

In this part the Second Mr. Wood has gelded from p. 1. to 44, and other pages too are wanting wherein are contain'd Trueths, but such as I entrusted nobody with the sight of but himself, whom I thought I might have entrusted wth my life. There are several papers that may cut my throate. I find too late, memento diffidere was a saying worthy of the sages. He hath also embezill'd the Index of it, q^d N.B.

It was stitch'd up when I sent it to him." "Novemb. 29, 1692."

In letters from Tanner to Aubrey, already mentioned, the former alludes to the detention of the latter's papers by Anthony à Wood. Requesting the loan of one of Aubrey's works, he says, "I shall scorn to be like Ant. Wood, viz. make use of your papers and acquaintance, and at last not afford you a good word : and again,

---

* Wood's *Athenæ Oxonienses*, by Bliss, vol. iv. col. 9.

† Lilly's *History of his Life and Times*, ed. 1774, p. 52.

‡ Copy, indorsed by Wood on the letter from Aubrey above quoted, and headed " Sent in a letter to Mr. Aubrey, to be com'unicated to Mr. Gadbury, in the latter end of Nov. 1692."

"You need not fear my playing the plagiary with your MSS., tho' I must excuse your jealousy of such a thing, Antony Wood having dealt so ungenteely by you."* The letters containing these passages were respectively written in May and December, 1693. Aubrey himself accused Wood of this offence in the following remarkable letter, dated nearly two years after the circumstance referred to had occurred. As they do not appear to have corresponded during the whole of that interval, it may have been a sort of reconciliatory letter. At all events the manner in which Aubrey mentions the subject is highly creditable to his feelings:

"Mr. Wood,   "Borstall, Sept. 2, 1694."

"I thought I should have heard from you ere this time. I have been ill ever since I came from Oxford, till within these five days, of a surfeit of peaches, &c.; so that I was faine to send to Kit White for a good Lusty Vomit. I $^{could}_{did}$ not eat a bitt of flesh for six days, but abstinence hath pretty well settled me again. Your unkindness and choleric humour was a great addition to my ilnes. You know I always loved you, and never thought I took paines enough to serve you; and I was told by severall at Oxford, and so the last yeare, that you can never afford me a good word. I desired you to give to the Museum my draught of Osney, which cost me xxs. when I was of Trin. Coll: 'twas donne by one Hesketh, a Hedge-Priest, who painted under Mr Dobson;† also I desired you to give the entertainment to the Queen at Bushells' Rocks; your Nephews and Neices will not value them. You have cutt out a matter of 40 pages out of one of my volumes, as also the index [was ever any body so unkind?] and I remember you told me coming from Heddington, that there were some things in it that would cutt my throat. I thought you so deare a friend that I might have entrusted my life in your hands; and now your unkindness doth almost break my heart. If you will returne these papers to me & the other things

* Originals, in the *Collection of Letters to Aubrey, ut supra.* (These are printed in *Letters from the Bodleian,* vol. ii. p. 164—169.)

† See ante, pp. 14, 51, as to this drawing of Osney Abbey. "Mr. Dobson" was the well known portrait painter, patronized by Vandyck and Charles I. He was appointed serjeant-painter to the king, and died in 1646. Neither the drawings of Osney, nor the other subject mentioned in this letter, are now to be found in the *Ashmolean Museum.*

. . . . . yᵒ may then have the Lives : I tooke Dʳ Gale's Life from his owne [mouth] . . . . erling's under his own hand.   I should be glad . . . . . , you shall be heartily welcome, and I will shew . . . . booke of this house, in parchment done in H. 6. and . . . . . this Estate granted to him by Edw. Confessor.*   I want Mʳ Lilly's Epitaph.   I would have you come the next week, for in a fort-night hence Sʳ J. A. goes into Glamorganshire, & will have me with him.   I have not been very fitt for riding, but I intend to spend 2 or 3 dayes . . . . . before Sir Jo. goes away.   You cannot imagine how much your unkindness vext and dis-composed me.   So God bless you.   Tuissimus, J. A."

" I would have you come hither as early as you can, because of perusing the MS. and seeing the gardens, for the afternoon will be taken up with good-fellowship." †

There is no evidence amongst the writings of Wood or Aubrey to show that the former ever made the latter any apology or explanation.   He died on the 28th November, 1695, in his 63rd, when Aubrey was in his 70th, year.   How strongly do the letter and the sentiments above quoted contrast with the splenetic and invidious language used by the author of *Athenæ Oxonienses*, who calls his traduced friend " a mere pretender to antiquities," and " little better than crazed."

About two years before Wood's death proceedings were taken against him for a libel on the Earl of Clarendon, for which he was fined and degraded, and the second volume of his *Athenæ Oxonienses*, containing the alleged libel, was publicly burnt.‡   It is stated by Hearne that the offensive passages in that work were inserted by Wood from Aubrey's notes,§ whence, according to Dr. Bliss, the former was punished for writings of which he was not the author ; and it is possible that Wood entertained some such feeling when he stated, in the article so often men-tioned, that Aubrey, " being exceedingly credulous, would stuff his many letters

---

* See a notice of the ancient chartulary here referred to in the note to page 23, ante.   Wood had visited Borstall and examined that curious manuscript in 1668.   (See his *Auto-biography*.)

† Original, in the *Ballard Collection, ut supra*.

‡ For a full account of these proceedings see Bliss's edition of Wood's *Athenæ Oxonienses*, vol. i.

§ *MS. Collections for* 1710 (quoted by Bliss, *ut supra*).

sent to A. W. with folliries, and misinformations, which sometimes would guid him
into the paths of errour." Still, it must be observed that the passages for which
Wood suffered were, like many other so-called *libels*, offensive only from their per-
tinence and truth; for Aubrey's statements, on which they are said to have been
founded, were evidently based upon good authority.* We are therefore compelled
to regard the testimony of Wood, with reference to Aubrey, as being quite at
variance with facts, as were also his perverted notices of the characters of Locke,
Ashmole, Bathurst, Wallis, and others.† The circumstances here adverted to, taken
in connexion with the former long and friendly correspondence of the two
biographers, prove that the account which Wood gave of Aubrey could only have
been written during the last three years of the former's life.

Few personal notices of Aubrey are to be found after those last referred to. On
the 20th of March, 1692-3, "about 11 at night, [he was] robbed and had 5 wounds
in his head,"‡ on which Dr. Garden condoled with him in his next letter. On the
5th of January following he had " an apoplectick fitt, circiter 4 h. P.M."§

In his *Miscellanies*‖ he says, "On the day of S\ John the Baptist, 1694, I accidentally was walking in the pasture behind Montague house,¶ it was 12 o'clock. I saw
there about two or three and twenty young women, most of them well habited, on
their knees very busy, as if they had been weeding. I could not presently learn
what the matter was; at last a young man told me, that they were looking for a
coal under the root of a plantain, to put under their head that night, and they

---

* Memoir of Judge Jenkins, in Aubrey's MS. *Lives of Eminent Men*, in the *Ashmolean Museum*. (This
memoir, so important in its bearing on the proceedings against Wood, was nevertheless omitted by the editors
of *Letters from the Bodleian*. It is, however, quoted by Bliss in his edition of Wood's *Athenæ Oxonienses*,
vol. i. p. clxix.)

† See D'Israeli's *Quarrels of Authors*, vol. ii. p. 275, *Biographia Britannica*, article *Ashmole*, and,
more especially, Malone's *Account of Aubrey*, in Boswell's *Shakespeare*, vol. ii. p. 695

‡ *Collection of Genitures, ut supra.*

§ Ibid.   ‖ Chapter on *Magick.*

¶ Montague House, now the British Museum, was at that time on the *northern verge of London*, bounded
by fields. So was it in 1790, when I was a boy. I often walked from Sadler's Wells, through *fields*, between
the Foundling Hospital on the north, and Bedford House and Montague House on the south, to Tottenham
Court *Road*. Dr. Stukeley, in his MS. diary, in my possession, describes the rural character of Queen-square,
and its vicinity, when he resided there in 1749.

should dream who would be their husbands. It was to be sought for that day and hour."

In 1695 Gibson's first edition of Camden's *Britannia* was published, in the preface to which he records his obligations to many literary men of the time, but omits the name of Aubrey. In his additions to Camden's remarks on *Wiltshire* he, however, quotes the account of Avebury from the *Monumenta Britannica*, respecting which place nothing had till then been published; and, moreover, in speaking of the different opinions concerning the origin and purposes of *Stonehenge*, the learned editor notices a theory "that it was a temple of the Druids long before the coming in of the Romans ; which," he adds, " Mr. John Aubrey, Fellow of the Royal Society, endeavours to prove in his Manuscript Treatise, entitled *Monumenta Britannica*."

In many other parts of the same edition of the *Britannia*, there are marginal references to " Mr John Aubrey's Manuscript Treatise, entitled Monumenta Britannica," to " Aubr. MS. Wilt.," and to " Letters from the learned and judicious Dr James Garden, Professor of Divinity at Aberdeen, to an ingenious gentleman of the Royal Society, Joh. Aubery of Easton-Pierce in Wiltshire, Esqr." Some of these passages may have been written by Tanner, who, as he states in the letters already referred to, assisted Gibson in his task, and who, in fact, borrowed the *Natural History of Wilts* to aid him therein. But, from his knowledge of the works referred to, Gibson was equally competent to write them, and there is reason to believe that, when his new edition of the " Britannia" appeared, Aubrey's *Monumenta Britannica* was either in his possession or in that of Churchill his publisher. In 1719 Mr. Churchill retained that manuscript,* and it continued in his family at least a century afterwards.

In 1696 Aubrey's *Miscellanies*† was published by Edward Castle, and dedicated by the Author "to the Right Honorable James Earl of Abingdon, Lord Chief Justice in Eyre of all His Majesty's Forests and Chaces on this side Trent,"

---

* Rawlinson's *Account of Aubrey*, prefixed to the *History of Surrey*.

† See page 2, *ante*.

as follows: " My Lord, When I enjoyed the contentment of solitude in your pleasant
walks and gardens at Lavington* the last summer, I reviewed several scattered
papers which had lain by me for several years ; and then presumed to think, that if
they were put together they might be somewhat entertaining : I therefore digested
them there in this order, in which I now present them to your Lordship . . .
. . . It was my intention to have finished my *Description of Wiltshire* † (half
finished already) and to have dedicated it to your Lordship : but my age is now
too far spent for such undertakings ; I have therefore devolved that task on my
countryman, Mr. Thomas Tanner, who hath youth to go through with it, and a
genius proper for such an undertaking.‡ Wherefore, I humbly beseech your
Lordship to accept of this small offering, as a grateful memorial of the profound
respect which I have for you, who have for many years taken me into your favour
and protection. My Lord, May the blessed angels be your careful guardians :
such are the prayers of your Lordship's most obliged and humble servant,

"JOHN AUBREY."

Our Antiquary made " many very considerable alterations, corrections, and additions" to this volume, apparently for the publication of a second edition. The copy
containing these notes belonged to Mr. Churchill, the bookseller already mentioned,
and with other copies was sold by auction, at the Queen's Head Tavern, Paternoster
Row, on Tuesday the 26th of July, 1720. The following letter from Aubrey to
Churchill was written on the first blank leaf of the volume : " Mr. Churchill. There is
a very pretty remark in the Athenian Mercury, concerning Apparitions, which I would
have inserted under this head. It is in vol. 17, numb. 25, Tuesday, June 1695.

---

* The old family mansion at this place, once the residence of nobles and men of learning, has, like many
other ancient houses of note, fallen to ruins, and, after various mutations into the dwelling and premises of the
farmer and even his labourer, has been effaced from the soil. Wood's account of Aubrey renders it probable that he often visited the Earl of Abingdon, at Lavington. The adjacent town of Market Lavington was
the birth-place and residence of his friend, Tanner.

† " Reposited in the Museum at Oxford."   This refers to the work printed by Sir Thomas Phillipps ;—the
Description of the North Division of Wiltshire : to which Aubrey, perhaps, intended to add a similar Description of the *South* division of the county.

‡ Aubrey's recent correspondence with Dr. Tanner had evidently led him to regard his new friend as his
literary executor, instead of Hooke, previously referred to.

Mr. Dunton,* at the Raven in Jewin Street, will help you to this Mercury, but yesterday he would not, his wife being newly departed. J. A."

In 1721 a second edition of the *Miscellanies* was published by "A. Bettesworth and J. Battley in Paternoster Row, J. Pemberton in Fleet Street, and E. Curll in the Strand," in which the above letter is printed; and which, besides some additions and corrections in various parts, contains the story of an apparition referred to by Aubrey as above mentioned.

The increasing age and bodily afflictions adverted to in Aubrey's correspondence, and especially the fit of apoplexy from which he suffered in the year 1694, were certain preludes to his decline and death. Probably another apoplectic fit was the immediate cause of his dissolution; at all events the suddenness of his decease isshewn by the fact that, within six days after the date of the above quoted letter, hewas buried in the ancient parish church of St. Mary Magdalene at Oxford. The entry in the register of burials stands thus:—" 1697 JOHN AUBERY A stranger was Buryed Jun. 7th."

The term " Stranger" merely implies that Aubrey was an out-parishioner, or extra-parochial person, for whose burial additional fees were charged. As a member of Trinity College he was probably interred in the south aile of the nave: where indeed so many distinguished members of that college were buried that until recently it was known as the "Trinity aile." There is no inscription, or other record than the register, to mark the place of his interment; nor is it probable that any sepulchral memorial of him was erected.

In 1719, Dr. Rawlinson stated in his *Memoir* that " several misfortunes" reduced Aubrey, in the latter part of his life, " to very low and mean circumstances, so that (as a Reverend Divine from Kington St. Michael's informed the Editor,) he was generously supported by the late Lady Long, of Draycot, in her own house, to which

---

* John Dunton was an eccentric and successful bookseller, from 1769 until within a few years of his death, which occurred in 1733. He carried on business at different places successively, but his shop generally bore the sign of the Black Raven. He wrote and published his " Life and Errors" (1705), wherein he records a variety of curious and interesting particulars of contemporary authors, printers, booksellers, &c. Many extracts from this volume may be found in Nichols's *Literary Anecdotes of the 18th Century;* especially an account of the origin, contents, and progress of the *Athenian Mercury*, which attained a great degree of popularity (vol. v. p. 67); and the Life and Errors, with selections from Dunton's other works, were reprinted in 1818, in two vols. 8vo.

L

he was going, on his return from London, when his journey and life were concluded at Oxford, where it is presumed he was buried; though neither the time of his Obit or his place of burial can be yet recovered."*

How far the statement that Aubrey was "supported" by Lady Long is correct, cannot now be ascertained. This Lady's husband, Colonel, afterwards Sir James Long, Bart., has been already mentioned. He frequently corresponded with Aubrey, and after his death, which occurred in 1692, his widow probably continued to the venerable antiquary that friendly patronage which he had previously enjoyed. The tradition of Aubrey being on his road to Draycot when he died rests entirely upon the authority of the passage above quoted, but it is most likely true.

Aubrey in his life-time fully anticipated some monument would be raised to mark his last resting-place. Amongst his papers are two suggestions, made at different times, for an Inscription to be placed on his tomb. In the first of these he describes himself briefly as the son and heir of Richard Aubrey of Easton-Pierse, adding, " Obiit A° D^{ni} 168 . . . die mensis . . . . . . A° Ætatis suæ 6 — ;"† shewing that he contemplated his demise much earlier than it occurred, for when that event took place he was in his 72nd year.

---

* After the publication of this Memoir, Dr. Rawlinson ascertained the place of Aubrey's burial; and wrote upon the margin of his own copy, now in the Bodleian Library, the following words: " Mr. John Aubrey died at Oxford, and was buried in St. Mary Magdalene Parish Church there, Octob. 1697." Though not precise as to the month, this note referred me to the right source of information respecting Aubrey's burial; and it is evident that no very extensive research was made by the various writers on the subject, from the time of Rawlinson to the present day, or it must otherwise have been long ago discovered. The portrait of Aubrey engraved by Vandergucht, which accompanied the learned Doctor's *Memoir*, was afterwards inscribed, below the name of Aubrey, " Obiit Oxon. Junii 7, 1697 ;" and with this addition impressions of the plate accompanied Manning and Bray's *History of Surrey*. This inscription, it will be observed, is not strictly correct; as the 7th of June was not the day of Aubrey's *death*, but of his *burial*. The majority of his biographers have been content to copy Dr. Rawlinson's printed statement on this point; though some of them state that he "died at Draycot," and others " on the road from Oxford to Draycot." Browne Willis appended a manuscript note to his copy of the memoir (now in the British Museum), as follows: " Buried in St. Michael's Church Oxon. in Jesus College Isle"; a statement not borne out by the registers of that church, and certainly erroneous. In the curious manuscript *Obituary* bequeathed by Sir William Musgrave, Bart. to the British Museum, the *year* of his death is correctly stated; the authority for it being merely indicated by the abbreviation " MS." which perhaps refers to the above mentioned note by Rawlinson. With these exceptions the question of time and place has till now remained in doubt, as it was left by the learned Doctor's Essay in 1719.

† *North Division of Wiltshire*, in the *Ashmolean Museum*.

The second proposed inscription, beneath a shield of the family arms, **Azure**, a chevron between three eagle's heads erased or, is as follows:—

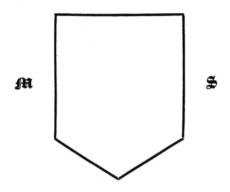

𝔍𝔬𝔥𝔞𝔫𝔫𝔢𝔰 𝔄𝔲𝔟𝔯𝔢𝔭
de Easton-Piers in Agro Wiltoñ,
Arm̃: Regalis Societatis Socius
infra situs est.
Obiit
Anno $\begin{cases} \text{Dñi.} \\ \text{Ætat.} \end{cases}$

" I wo^d desire that this Inscription sho^d be a stone of white Mble. about the bigness of a royal sheet of paper, scilicet, about 2 foot square. Mr. Reynolds of Lambeth, Stonecutter, (Foxhall,) who married Mr. Elias Ashmole's Widow, will ^{sell}/_{help} me to a Marble as square as an imperial sheet of paper for 8 shillings." *

John Aubrey died intestate: and Letters of Administration to his effects were granted, on the 18th of December 1697, to his surviving brother, William.† In the record of the circumstance in the Prerogative Office, Doctors' Commons, John is described as " late of Broad Chalk in the county of Wilts, Bachelor."

William Aubrey lived until 1707. He seems to have been on very affectionate

---

* Written on a fly leaf at the end of Aubrey's *Interpretation of Villare Anglicanum*, in the *Ashmolean Museum*.

† Thomas, his younger brother, died many years before. (See Pedigree, p. 24.)

terms with his brother, and occasionally assisted him in his antiquarian researches.*
He resided at Kington St. Michael, where he died, unmarried; and was buried in
the parish church on the 29th of October. His circumstances appear to have been
straitened, for his "principal creditor, Thomas Stokes," took out administration of
his goods and chattels, on the 24th of November following his death. If William
Aubrey had preserved any of his brother's personal or literary documents, they
were most probably destroyed by those into whose hands they afterwards passed.

THE PRECEDING narrative, and the varied memoranda of Aubrey himself, together
with those of his contemporaries, which have been quoted from numerous manuscript and printed works, cannot fail to afford ample evidence and elucidation of the
prominent characteristics of the man. They also furnish many striking features of
the tone and temper of an age which was peculiar, and deserving of remark, for the
illiteracy, superstition, and besotted infatuation of even the higher classes of society.
In spite of the writings and example of such men as Camden, Bacon, and Shakspere, who preceded the Aubrey era, the greater part of the seventeenth century may
be classed as part of the "dark ages." The foundation of the Royal, and some other
literary and scientific societies, was the advent of improvement in the public mind,
and, though their effects were not immediate or remarkable, they unquestionably
opened new roads to social intercourse and mental emulation. Had Aubrey lived and
associated with Dr. Stukeley, and the other founders of the Society of Antiquaries, and
the Egyptian Society, we may be assured that both his writings and his life would
have presented many features, dissimilar to those shown by the evidence here
adduced. It is but reasonable to infer that, had all his private manuscripts been
preserved, they would have afforded much additional information relating to himself
and his contemporaries, as well as to many places and things, which would in the
present day be highly interesting.

In reviewing the personal or domestic characteristics of JOHN AUBREY, by the

---

* See *North Division of Wiltshire*, (printed by Sir Thomas Phillipps,) part ii. pp. 2, 82, and a letter
from Tanner in the *Collection of Letters to Aubrey, ut supra*, vol. ii.

aid of such materials as are accessible, the qualities most conspicuous are his frank and candid simplicity, combined with a natural warmth and kindness of heart: a disposition, however, which was accompanied (as is too often the case) with a certain degree of incapacity for the active business of life, and a proportionate love of literary ease or indolence. Less fortunate in pecuniary affairs than his birth and station in life had led him to anticipate, he was always involved in debt after the demise of his father, and consequently became harassed and oppressed by litigation.

Aubrey was an affectionate relative, a kind and indulgent master,* and a sincere, enthusiastic, and forbearing friend : qualities which must have endeared him to all his acquaintance. His sympathies for Hobbes as well as Wood led Aubrey to feel acutely the injury inflicted on the latter by Bishop Fell, who, contrary to the author's wish, not only caused his *History of the University of Oxford* to be translated into Latin, but altered and mutilated it in many parts, and more especially in the notice of the "philosopher of Malmesbury." Here is one of Aubrey's many epistles to Wood upon the subject : " I received your kind letter wth Dr Fell's insertions concerning my countryman M^r Th. Hobbes, & sent you an answer to it, and . . . . of my delivering it to him (who remembers him very kindly to y^o), and that he wo^d desire y^o to write a letter of complaint to him of it, and he will vindicate himself in print against ye D^r, at ye end of a book he is now printing, viz. the translation of Homer's Odysseys. I have not since heard from y^o, so that whether y^o received my letter I am doubtful. I showed it to Sr Chr. Wren & Dr Twisse (who remembers him to y^o) *cum multis aliis,* Virtuosis; who all *(uno ore)* cry out of the injustice used against y^o, and say again (amongst others Mr Dugdale & Mr Ashmole) that y^o have no way so good to cleare yourselfe, as to print a sheet here in London of ye D^{rs} foystings, to be bound up wth yor book. Dr Twisse is sufficiently nettled (as he haz reason) and is glad to heare of such a revenger." This was dated April, 1674 ; and he renews the subject, urging most strongly an explanation on the part of Wood, in several

---

* In a letter to Wood, 1668, Aubrey urges him to recommend his " beloved servant, Robinet, to wait on Mr President" (Bathurst, of Trinity College), " such being the height of his desires." He further adds, " I could prefer him to the E. of Worcester, or Pembroke, but Oxford is the place he loves, and where he could make out a better livelyhood." In subsequent letters he sends his " love to Robinet."—*Ballard Collection, ut supra.*

other letters, written in the same year. " Your book," he says, " is generally very well received, but would have been better, had not yᵉ Dean embittered it, so much and so often, wᵗʰ his gall and spleen."*

Except in this instance, Aubrey was not a partizan in any of the literary quarrels of his time. Unlike Hobbes and Wallis, Wren and Flamsteed, Hooke and Newton, his name does not appear to have been immediately involved in any personal or literary dispute.

In the age in which he lived credulity and superstition might be especially expected to accompany such a warm, enthusiastic temperament as Aubrey's; and, but for his innate good sense, acuteness, and discrimination, the absurd delusions of astrology would have exercised more potent influence over his works and actions than they appear to have done.

Aubrey, it may be presumed, received as good an education as was usually imparted by the tutors and colleges of his age. The course appears to have embraced the classics, a general knowledge of algebra, geometry, mathematics, natural history, &c.; but he never became eminent as a *scholar* or *man of science*. His *Idea of Education* shows that, although he did not undervalue the advantages of mere erudition, he felt the necessity of a more *practical* system of instruction than he had himself received, in order to prepare a youth for the business and general pursuits of the world.

His loyalty to the House of Stuart was no doubt sincere; but it is displayed rather by invectives against the tyranny of the Puritans than by any expressions of regard for their ill-fated but misguided victim,—Charles the First,—or his profligate successor. Religious topics he seldom appears to have adverted to. He was a Protestant; and he records his devout acknowledgments to the Almighty for preservation from many dangers. (Vide ante, pp. 18, 19.)

Aubrey's love of literature, of science, and of antiquarian research and illustration, the interest he felt in all projects for local or national improvements, and in matters relating to the mechanical and useful arts, together with his zeal for the

---

* Originals in the *Ballard Collection, ut supra.*

welfare and advancement of societies, and public bodies, instituted with similar views, are proved by numerous passages in his writings. His *Lives of Eminent Men** especially, have many memoranda showing his desire to advocate and promote such objects.

His easy and familiar *style of composition* has been already illustrated by the extracts from his writings in the preceding pages. It is certainly peculiar, and almost unique. Notwithstanding their liveliness and freedom, his productions have much less vulgarity and coarseness than those of many of his contemporaries ; but they are occasionally disfigured by uncouth words of Latin derivation, now long since obsolete. His *orthography* is comparatively pure and modern. It is true, precision in the orthography of *names* was not then practised or studied ; hence, though he generally spelt his own name " Aubrey," on some occasions he wrote it " Awbrey." He frequently used the monogram J. A. (formed by a J. within, and crossing the horizontal line of, the letter A.) instead of a signature at full ; sometimes he Latinized the name, " *Albericus* ;" and in one letter to Anthony à Wood he quaintly signs " *Jo. Gregorius*," perhaps with reference to his birth upon *St. Gregory's Day*. His *handwriting* varies considerably. In later life, and in all of his most hurried memoranda, it is very small and illegible ; but his more elaborate and important manuscripts are in a bold and plain character.

Although we have not any satisfactory data to mark or define his general personal figure and appearance,† we may infer from the *portrait* accompanying this volume that his features were manly, bold, expressive, and intelligent. The nose, mouth, forehead, and eyes show that the face was symmetrical and fine, and, therefore, calculated to make a good bust or picture. The monstrous and barbarous wig, however, not only disfigured the human countenance, but, like a bad and disgusting frame to a beautiful picture, was calculated to deteriorate and degrade the gem it enshrined.

---

* See volume ii. pp. 203, 432, 475, 502. Also his *Faber Fortunæ*, noticed in chap. v. of this Memoir.

† In noticing the " squeaking voice" of Dr. Kettle, Aubrey says, " they were wont to mock me with this." (*Lives of Eminent Men*, vol. ii. p. 422.) This corroborates the allusion of Henry Coley (ante, p. 48) to " an Impediment in ye Native's speech." From a note to his *Life of Milton* we learn that Aubrey was " of middle stature." He was particularly minute in describing the personal appearance of those of whom he wrote, and perhaps attached some importance to the advantages of a handsome face and figure.

Aubrey distinctly mentions at least *three* original *Portraits* of himself.   The first was taken in 1656, when he was thirty years of age.   He does not name the artist, but merely states that a picture of him, painted at that age, was, in 1671, in the possession of the widow of his friend, Lord Charles Seymour.*   It may have been the work of the celebrated Samuel Cooper, who is known to have painted his portrait.   Indeed, if this early picture were not by him, it must be held to constitute a *fourth* in the present list, as the artists of two others are known.   In a letter to John Ray he writes: "London, Oct. 22, 1691. Sir, When I was lately at Oxford I gave several things to the Musæum, which was lately robbed, since I wrote to you.   Among other things my picture in miniature, by Mr S. Cowper, (which at an auction yields 20 Guineas,) and Archbishop Bancroft's, by Hillyard, the famous Illuminer in Q. Elizabeth's time."†   To which Ray replied, " You write that the Museum at Oxford was rob'd, but do not say whether your noble present was any part of the losse.   Your picture done in miniature by Mr Cowper is a thing of great value.   I remember so long ago as I was in Italy, & while he was yet living, any piece of his was highly esteemed there ; & for that kind of painting he was esteemed the best artist in Europe."‡   No portrait of Aubrey by Cooper, nor any portrait of Archbishop Bancroft, is now in the Ashmolean Museum, nor is the fact of such pictures having been there formerly on record.   They were probably stolen, as mentioned in the above letters.§

Respecting the identity of two other portraits, there is no doubt.   One of these

---

* " My Ld. Ch. Seymour had my picture, ætat. 30, which his lady now hath."—Note, dated 1671, on title page of *Monumenta Britannica*.   The nobleman here alluded to (who died in 1665) is the same individual mentioned as the Honourable Mr. Seymour in p. 30, ante.   Since writing the note * in p. 16, I have been led to conclude that the " Mr. Ch. Seymour" there noticed amongst the friends of Aubrey, is also the same person as the " Ld. Ch. Seymour" here named.   The reader is therefore desired to cancel the note referred to.   In enumerating his distinguished friends, Aubrey inserted his lordship's name, although at that time he had been dead more than fifteen years.   He described him as *Mr.* Seymour, as he had only been Lord Seymour of Troubridge a year before his death.

† Printed in Ray's *Philosophical Letters*, 8vo. 1718, p. 251 ; and in Aubrey's *History of Surrey*, vol. v. p. 408.

‡ Original annexed to Aubrey's *Natural History of Wilts*, in the *Ashmolean Museum*.

§ If the picture painted in Aubrey's thirtieth year was identical with that by Cooper, it follows that, between 1671 and 1691, it had been returned by Lady Seymour.

was drawn by William Faithorne the elder* (an artist well known by his finely engraved portraits), in the year 1666, when Aubrey was forty years of age. This has been engraved several times, but I can confidently assert that the print accompanying the present memoir is a more faithful copy of the original than any previously published. The drawing, which is in the Ashmolean Museum, Oxford, is executed in Indian ink, in a careful and beautiful manner, with the flesh slightly coloured. It is in an old black frame, and has an inscription beneath, which (though partly pasted over in the process of mounting) may still be read, as follows : " Mr. John Aubrey, R.S.S. 1666. Ætatis 40."

The author intended to have this drawing engraved for publication in his *Monumenta Britannica,* as appears by another part of the note upon the title-page of the work already quoted:—" My brother hath the picture that Mr. Faithorn drew in black and white, A° 1666, in order to engrave it for this book." But the contemplated publication being deferred, he, about twenty years afterwards, had another portrait drawn by David Loggan,† who was also an engraver: and it is evident that the latter drawing was intended to be engraved to accompany his *Natural History of Wiltshire.* It is so expressly mentioned, not only in the curious Will printed in page 60, but also on the manuscript of the work itself, as follows :—" Anno 1686. Ætatis 60. Mr. David Loggan the graver, drew my picture, in black and white, in order to be engraved, which is still in his hands."

No plate from either of these drawings had been engraved until 1719 ; when

---

* WILLIAM FAITHORNE was born in London, but it is not known in what year. He died in 1691. It is said that he studied the art of painting portraits in crayons at Paris. His engravings, which are chiefly portraits, are executed almost entirely with the graver, in a clear, free style. Many of them are of admirable execution ; and good impressions from some are scarce and valuable. At the time he drew Aubrey's portrait, he was carrying on a considerable trade in Italian, Dutch, and English prints, near Temple Bar, where he had established himself as an engraver and printseller.—Bryan's *Dictionary of Painters and Engravers.*

† DAVID LOGGAN was born at Dantzic about the year 1630. He came to England before the Restoration, and was first employed in engraving views of the public buildings of the University of Oxford. He also drew and engraved a series of views of the colleges, &c. in Cambridge (folio, 1688), which, with those of the sister University, are highly interesting. His works are generally executed with the graver, in a neat, but formal style.—Bryan's *Dictionary of Painters and Engravers.*

M

Michael Vander Gucht copied that of Faithorne, in line, for Aubrey's *History of Surrey*, 8vo. which was published in that year by Dr. Rawlinson. This bears the inscription "John Aubrey, Esq. F.R.S. M. V^{der} Gucht Sculp." Impressions of the same plate, printed on folio paper, and with the words "Obiit Oxon. Junii 7, 1697," added to the Inscription, were prefixed to the second volume of Manning and Bray's *History of Surrey*, 1809.

The next engraved portrait of Aubrey was a frontispiece to J. Caulfield's *Oxford Cabinet*, a 4to. volume published in 1797, containing a few of Aubrey's *Lives of Eminent Men*. This, which is in stipple, and larger than Vander Gucht's head, has beneath it the family shield and crest of Aubrey; also the name "John Aubrey, Esq. F.R.S."; but no artist's name. In the arms, the eagle's heads (both in the shield and crest) are incorrectly turned to the sinister side; but I have an impression of the plate with the arms corrected by the engraver, and with the additional words, "Published by J. Caulfield, Jany. 1. 1798."

Another portrait deserving especial notice was engraved by Francis Bartolozzi, for Malone, from a copy of Faithorne's Drawing, purposely made by Silvester Harding. It was never published, and impressions are exceedingly scarce; indeed only two or three proofs were probably taken. As it is a fine specimen by a justly celebrated engraver, it would have gratified me to have substituted impressions of that plate for those prefixed to this memoir.*

A fourth portrait was engraved by T. Cook, for Malcolm's *Lives of Topographers and Antiquaries* (4to. 1815), and there is also an unpublished etching by Mrs. Dawson Turner, of Great Yarmouth, Norfolk. All of these are from the Ashmolean picture.

---

* Mr. G. P. Harding, an artist of talent, who has devoted many years to copying fine old historical portraits, has the only proof of the plate I have ever seen. Knowing that it had been executed for the late Edmund Malone, and intended by him for his last edition of Shakspere's works, I instituted inquiries, through the medium of the *Gentleman's Magazine*, and of persons who were connected with the annotator on Shakspere, for the unpublished plate, but without success. Some of Mr. Malone's books, &c. were deposited in the Bodleian library, Oxford, and others in the public library at Dublin, to each of which establishments I applied in vain. The engraving is noticed in Granger's *Biographical History of England*, vol. v. p. 272 (8vo. edition of 1824).

Chap. V.

IN the following brief account of Aubrey's literary papers I propose to describe the contents and present state of them, in the order marked by himself, as already given (page 20).

The greater part of these are in the Ashmolean Museum, at Oxford. Aubrey's gift to that establishment has been already mentioned; and the circumstance is recorded, in a prominent and appropriate manner, by the following inscription, in letters of gold, upon a blue ground, over the doorway to the library of the Museum.

" LIBRI IMPRESSI ET MANUSCRIPTI E DONIS CLARISS. VIRORUM D. ELIÆ ASHMOLE ET MARTIN LISTER: QUIBUS NON PAUCOS ADDIDIT VIR INDUSTRIUS NEC INFIME DE RE ANTIQUARIA ET PHYSICA PROMERITUS, D. JOHANNES AUBREY DE EASTON PIERCE APUD WILTONENSES ARM. ET SOC: REG: SOCIUS."*

His manuscripts do not appear to have sustained any material injury since they were first deposited there: along with them are some writings in small quarto, on musical subjects, by Mercator; and a beautiful breviary, which belonged to Sir Thomas Pope. These formed part of Aubrey's collection; and, in addition, there are two folio manuscript volumes relating to Dr. Dee, preserved in the same closet, which have been considered † as part of his gift to the Museum; whereas they were in fact presented by Edward Llhwyd. One of those volumes is

---

* " The printed and manuscript books bestowed by those most famous men, Elias Ashmole and Martin Lister; to which not a few were added by that industrious man, and no mean deserver in things relating to antiquity, John Aubrey, of Easton Peirce, in Wiltshire, Esq. and F.R.S."—*Translation in Biographia Britannica.*

† By Warton and Huddesford, in their edition of *Anthony à Wood's Life.* 8vo. 1772.

chiefly in the hand-writing of Dr. Dee, and the other contains some materials,
collected by Elias Ashmole, for a life of that once noted astrologer.   Nearly the
whole of the ancient coins, which were given to the Museum by Aubrey, still
form part of its collection.   They consisted of thirty-seven Roman brass specimens,
principally of the Lower Empire; and fourteen matrices for Roman coins; most
of which were found at Edington, in the parish of Moorlinch, Somersetshire.   Only
five of the latter remain, and these, with a few of the former, are exhibited
in one of the glass cases.   Aubrey also gave to the Museum a fragment of a
Roman pavement from Farley Castle, Wiltshire;* but this, according to a memo-
randum on an old manuscript catologue of the collection, was subsequently
removed, though for what reason it is difficult to say, into the Medical Professor's Cabinet; which was in a separate building.

Aubrey's manuscripts, given to the Museum, could hardly have amounted to
more than thirty volumes; therefore, according to the Register of Benefactions
(quoted in page 63), he must have presented also about fifty volumes of printed
books.   Unlike the manuscripts, these have always been mixed and confounded
with the general collection; no separate list of them appears to have been made;
and they are only to be identified by the autograph of the donor, which appears
inside the covers of some of them, or the inscription, " Musei Ashmoleani Ex dono
clarissimi authoris," † written upon others.   Amongst the volumes thus traced are
several containing Popish Plot pamphlets, and similar ephemeral publications.

The following account of the AUBREY MANUSCRIPTS may be useful to future
antiquaries and biographers: whilst it will tend to confirm and exemplify the
opinions herein given of his personal industry and literary merits.

I.   "ANTIQUITIES OF WILTSHIRE, AFTER THE METHOD OF SIR W. DUGDALE'S
DESCRIPTION OF WARWICKSHIRE.   2 PARTS, IN FOL."   [*In the Ashmolean
Museum.*]

Incidental notices of this work, especially of the manner in which it was first
undertaken by the writer in 1659, and of its elaborate execution, will be found in

* Camden's *Britannia*, by Gibson, (1695), note in col. 105, quoting Aubrey as the authority.

† These words are inscribed on the copy of Aubrey's *Miscellanies*, given by him to the Museum.

previous pages of the present memoir. It consists of two volumes, folio, bound in vellum; with the title, "An Essay Towards the Description of the North Division of Wiltshire. By me John Aubrey, of Easton Pierse." During the author's life it was lent successively to Wood and to Tanner, and quoted in Gibson's edition of Camden's *Britannia*. Aubrey alludes to it under the titles, the *Description of Wiltshire*, and the *Antiquities of Wiltshire*; but never by its full title, as here given. He speaks of it in the Dedication of his *Miscellanies*, as being " half finished already," and "reposited in the Ashmolean Museum at Oxon."

The "Introduction" to this manuscript was printed entire in a very scarce and curious pamphlet, published in 1714, and which is deserving of particular notice. This little work, often erroneously quoted as "AUBREY's" *Miscellanies*, bears the following title:—"*Miscellanies on several curious subjects*: now first publish'd from their respective originals. London, Printed for E. Curll, at the Dial and Bible, over against St. Dunstan's Church in Fleet Street, 1714." (8vo. pp. 88).* The title page has a small medallion portrait, which in the catalogue of the Stourhead Library is said to represent Aubrey. This is evidently erroneous; as is also a manuscript note I have seen, stating that the volume was edited by Hearne, and that the portrait is intended for Anthony à Wood. The present remarks are intended to correct an erroneous statement made in the *Essay on Topography*, (p. xl.) published by the Wiltshire Topographical Society, in which the volume above referred to is confounded with Aubrey's *Miscellanies*.

From the *Introduction* to the volume by Aubrey, now under consideration, it may be expedient to quote a few passages which are intimately connected with his biography, and also with the Topography of Wiltshire. "I am heartily sorry I did not set down the Antiquities of these parts sooner, for since the Time aforesaid [1659] many Things are irrecoverably lost. In former Days the Churches and great Houses hereabouts did so abound with Monuments and Things remarkable, that it would have

---

* Besides the Introduction to Aubrey's *North Division of Wiltshire*, the volume contains the charge, answer, and sentence, in the prosecution of Anthony à Wood for his alleged libel on Lord Clarendon; also five letters on various matters of antiquity by Ashmole, Plot, Langbaine, and Selden; and five others, on similar subjects, addressed to Aubrey by Andrew Paschal, John Lydall, and E. G. [Edmund Gibson?]

deterr'd an Antiquary from undertaking it." After a review of the state of the
northern part of Wiltshire before the Roman Invasion, and under the dynasties
of the Romans, Saxons, Normans, &c. successively, he states that "in the time of
Henry VIII. this country was a lovely Champain, as that about Sherston and
Cotswold; very few Enclosures, unless near Houses. My Grandfather Lyte did
remember when all between Cromhall (at Eston) and Castle Comb was so, when
Easton, Yatton, and Comb, did intercommon together. In my remembrance much
hath been enclos'd, and every year more and more is taken in. Anciently the *Leghs*
(now corruptly called Sleights), i. e. Pastures, were noble large grounds, as yet the
demesne lands at Castle Combe are. So likewise in his remembrance was all
between Kington St. Michael and Draycot Cerne common fields. There was a
world of labouring people maintained by the plough, as yet in Northamptonshire,
&c. There were no rates for the poor in my Grandfather's dayes; but for Kington
St Michael (no small parish) the Church-ale at Whitsuntide did the business". He
then traces the derivation of the term Church-ale, and, after noticing the religious
festivals of the times referred to, says, "Such joy and merriment was every Holyday;
which days were kept with great solemnity and reverence. These were the days
when England was famous for the Grey Goose Quills." . . . . . "This country was
full of Religious houses. Old Jacques (who lived where Charles Hadnam did) could
see from his house the Nuns of the Priory of St. Mary's (juxta Kington) come forth
into the Nymph-Hay, with their Rocks and Wheels, to spin, and with their sewing
work. He would say that he hath told three score and ten; tho' of Nuns there
were not so many; but in all, with Lay-sisters, as Widows, Old maids, and young
Girls, there might be such a number. This was a fine way of breeding up young
women, who are led more by example than precept, and a good retirement for
widows and grave single women, to a civil, virtuous, and holy Life." It concludes
thus: "This searching after Antiquities is a wearisome task. I wish I had gone
through all the Church monuments. The records at London I can search gratis.
Though of all studies I take the least delight in this, yet methinks I am carried on
with a kind of Œstrum; for nobody else hereabout hardly cares for it, but rather
makes a scorn of it. But methinks it shews a kind of gratitude and good nature, to

revise the memories and memorials of the pious and charitable Benefactors long since dead and gone. Eston-Pierse, April 28, 1670."*

This work, as already mentioned (ante, p. 2), has been published at the expense of Sir Thomas Phillipps, Bart.,† who however acknowledges that his edition was printed from a transcript, and that the proof sheets were not compared with the original. The omission of Aubrey's original drawings seriously depreciates the printed copy. Amongst these are some interesting sketches of Kington St. Michael, shewing the church, with the spire, which was then standing; and the adjoining buildings. The passages in *Domesday Book* relating to Kington and Langley have been copied with great care and literal accuracy, and are preserved in the manuscript referred to.

All previous writers have omitted to distinguish this work from that by Aubrey, on the *Natural History of Wiltshire* (see Article III.) Warton and Huddesford mention only the latter; and their statement has been copied in every succeeding notice, excepting that in the *Biographical Dictionary* of the Society for the Diffusion of Useful Knowledge, by Mr. Stanesby, who was led to conjecture that there were two works on Wiltshire written by Aubrey.

II.—" MONUMENTA BRITANNICA. 3 PARTS. FOL."

All my attempts to trace the manuscript of this important work have failed. I possess, however, an abstract of it, which was made for me, from one more copious, in the Bodleian Library, Oxford. The latter was copied by Richard Gough, the Topographer, from a manuscript in the possession of the Rev. Mr. Hutchins, of

---

* As early as 1716 this introduction was quoted by the author of a curious essay well known to Topographers, viz. *A Little Monument to the once famous Abbey and Borough of Glastonbury*; published in Hearne's *History of Glastonbury* (1722).

† In two parts, small 4to. The first was printed by J. Davy, Queen Street, Seven Dials, in 1821, with the title, " Aubrey's Collections for Wilts, Part I." and the second in 1838, with the full title, " An Essay Towards the Description of the North Division of Wiltshire. By me John Aubrey, of Easton Pierse. Typis Medio-Montanis, Impressit C. Gilmour, 1838." The first part was printed when Sir Thomas was abroad, and he admits, " not so accurately as I could have desired. To this second part therefore I have added the list of Errata, by which the possessors of the work will be able to correct their 1st part." Unfortunately, these Errata do not appear in the copies of the second part which I have seen, nor have the promised " Appendix of Plates and Descriptions of Arms" yet made their appearance.

Wareham, in Dorsetshire (the learned historian of that county), which copy was, in its turn, abridged from the original by Aubrey.

At the time of Aubrey's death the original work belonged to Awnsham Churchill, an opulent London bookseller and publisher, at the end of the seventeenth and early part of the eighteenth centuries, and it remained in the possession of his descendants until the year 1819.

Churchill was the last person with whom we find Aubrey in communication (vide ante p. 72). He published Gibson's edition of Camden's *Britannia* (1695), and it is not improbable that Aubrey deposited the *Monumenta Britannica* with him for the purpose of publication; or it may have been left in his custody, after the completion of the *Britannia*, by one of the literary friends of Aubrey, who must have had recourse to it for the improvement of that work: the latter supposition is strengthened by a note in Warton's *Life of Bathurst* (8vo. 1761, p. 151). Dr. Rawlinson, in his *Memoir* of the author (1719), states that the manuscript was at that time *said to be* in Mr. Churchill's hands. The wealthy bookseller purchased the manor of Henbury, near Wimborne, in Dorsetshire, in 1704; was member of Parliament for Dorchester in 1709; and ultimately died unmarried.*

The manuscript afterwards became the property of his nephew and representative, Awnsham Churchill, of Henbury; and in 1755 the Rev. John Hutchins, who resided in the vicinity, " made a faithful abstract of it, with copies of the rude sketches, while it was lent to him for the use of his excellent history of Dorsetshire."†

The original was, perhaps, inaccessible to Gough, for in October 1769 he made his transcript or abridgment from Hutchins's. He evidently thought very highly of the work, and in his *British Topography*,‡ published in 1780, and afterwards in his edition of Camden's *Britannia*,§ he refers to it with much commendation. He states that the original was then in the possession of Awnsham Churchill, Esq. of Henbury, who he calls a *son* of Awnsham Churchill, the bookseller.

At a very early period of my architectural and antiquarian studies, my attention

---

* See an article by an old correspondent of the *Gentleman's Magazine* (1783), quoted in Nichols's *Literary Anecdotes of the* 18th *Century*, (ed. 1812), vol. i. p. 150, note.

† Ibid.　　　　‡ Preface, p. xiii. and vol. ii. pp. 369, 370.　　　　§ Wiltshire, p. 145, note.

was forcibly drawn to this work, in consequence of the notice which it had received from Gough and other writers; and accordingly, in 1814, I was induced to procure the copy I have already mentioned from that of Gough; which, on his death, had been deposited in the Bodleian Library, at Oxford. In 1817 I lent the volume to the late Sir Richard Colt Hoare, who was so much pleased with its contents that he applied to Mr. William Churchill, of Henbury (a son of Awnsham Churchill the younger), who then possessed the original, and by his kindness procured the loan of it, for the purposes of his work on *Ancient Wiltshire.** Sir Richard made copious extracts from the manuscript, chiefly of the parts relating to Wiltshire; and these, which, excepting Mr. Hutchins's, appear to be the only direct transcripts ever made from Aubrey's work, still remain in the library at Stourhead, Wiltshire. Sir Richard Hoare added some manuscript notes, in illustration of the text, to my abstract, and these have been since augmented by myself, by Dr. Sherwen, of Bath, and also by others.

Since 1819, when Sir Richard Hoare referred to the *Monumenta* as being in the possession of William Churchill, Esq., I have not been able to learn its history. On the death of the latter gentleman, many years ago, his son William sold Henbury, with portions of his father's library, and resided himself in London; but I have failed to ascertain from the representatives, either of those who conducted the sale, or of the principal purchaser, whether Aubrey's manuscript was then disposed of. If retained by Mr. Churchill, it perhaps formed part of his library in London, which on his death passed to his cousin Sir Charles Greville. That gentleman is also dead, and his brother, the Earl of Warwick, who inherited his library, is not aware that the manuscript is in his collection, either in London, or at the Castle of Warwick.

The work bore the title, " Monumenta Britannica, or a Miscellanie of British Antiquities;" and, according to Gough and Sir Richard C. Hoare, it consisted of four thin folio volumes, of about 100 pages each; the contents being arranged as follows :—

* See vol. ii. p. 57 of that work.

N

PART (OR VOL.) I. Chap. 1. Templa Druidum, including a review of Stonehenge, a particular account of Avebury; and notices of Druidical monuments in various parts of Great Britain.*—2. Mantissa de Religione et Moribus Druidum; from several ancient authors.—3. An Apparatus of Bards.—4. Four of Dr. Garden's Letters to Aubrey respecting Celtic Monuments, one of them being the letter printed in *Archæologia*, vol. i. p. 312.

PART II. Chap. 1. Of Camps.—2. Old Castles, or Castella.—3. Military Architecture.—4. Roman Towns.—5. Pittes.—6. Hornes.

PART III. Chap. 1. Barrows.—2. Urnes.—3. Sepulchres.—4. Ditches.—5. High Wayes.—6. Roman Pavements.—7. Coins.—8. Embanking and Draining.

PART IV. (which was entitled ΣΤΡΩΜΑΤΑ sive Miscellanea). Chap. 1. Chronologia Architectonica.—2. Chronologia Graphica.—3. Chronologia Aspidologica.—4. Chronologia Vestiaria.—5. Weights and Measures.†—6. Prices of Corne.†—7. Diversities of Standards or Values of Money.†—8. Nouvelles; natural and artificial things, by whom, and when, brought into England.—9. The proportion of the several languages, ingredients of our present English.†

There seems to have been a fifth part, containing remarks on Day-fatality, Omens, Dreams, &c.; but these were, no doubt, embodied in the volume Aubrey published with the title of *Miscellanies*, and therefore cannot be regarded as a portion of the *Monumenta Britannica*. The work, as we have seen (ante p. 66), was lent to many of the author's friends, who all thought highly of it: some manuscript notes were added by John Evelyn, and Dr. Thomas Gale, and are favourably

* This chapter constituted by far the most important and valuable part of the work. It bore the motto, from Cicero, *De Divinatione*, " Quis est, quem non moveat clarissimis monumentis testata consignataque antiquitas?" which, from its peculiar application to the great temple at Avebury, was adopted by Sir Richard Hoare, and prefixed to his account of that monument. It is evident from Aubrey's correspondence that, partly in compliance with a desire expressed by Dugdale, he at one time contemplated printing this chapter separately. Tanner, however, who refers to some "proposals" for printing it, strongly urges him to " abridge it *all*, and print it in about forty sheets, which," he says, " will make a very fair octavo or quarto." (*Letters from the Bodleian*, vol. ii. p. 170. See also several passages in the *Original Letters to and from Aubrey* in the *Ashmolean Museum*, and *Bodleian Library, ut supra*.)

† Gough states that the manuscript was deficient in these chapters.

spoken of by Warton and Gough. It was dedicated to the Earl of Pembroke, to whom also a work to be noticed next,—the *Natural History of Wiltshire*,—was inscribed; and the Will, printed in p. 60, shows that Aubrey proposed to incorporate the two works in one publication.

The *Monumenta Britannica* had its origin in the command given by King Charles the Second to the author, to print an account of Avebury (vide ante p. 39). The nature of its contents were not, however, made public till 1695, when Gibson's edition of the *Britannia* appeared; wherein Aubrey's theory respecting Stonehenge is expressly quoted, together with an abridgment of his description of Avebury.* After that date the work was alluded to in the *Memoirs* of Aubrey, prefixed to his *History of Surrey* (1719) and *Miscellanies* (2nd ed. 1721). Dr. Stukeley published his volume on *Abury* in 1743, but does not allude to Aubrey's remarks upon that temple, though he can hardly be supposed to have been ignorant of them. In p. 32, he refers to "Mr. Aubrey's manuscript notes, printed with Camden's *Britannia*." In his *Itinerarium Curiosum*, vol. ii. p. 169, speaking of the stone circle at Stanton Drew, in Somersetshire, he says, "Mr. Aubrey, that indefatigable searcher-out of antiquities, is the first that has observed it." The *Monumenta* was particularly noticed, as already mentioned, by Warton (in his *Life of Bathurst*, 1761), by Gough, and by Sir Richard C. Hoare; and it appears that Francis Perry published some rude etchings from the sketches by Aubrey, in the first chapter of Part IV., illustrating "the several styles of windows, &c. in England." These, it is stated, he executed "while Mr. Hutchins's abstract was in the hands of one of his London friends." †

---

* It is singular that the learned Editor of the *Britannia* does not mention Aubrey, amongst the many correspondents to whom, in his *Preface*, he acknowledges obligations.

† Nichols's *Literary Anecdotes of the 18th Century* (ed. 1812), vol. i. p. 150, note; and Gough's *British Topography*, vol. ii. p. 370, note. Perry's etchings are to be found in his volume, entitled, "A Series of English Medals," 4to. 1762.

III.—" MEMOIRES OF NATURALL REMARQUES IN WILTS. 2 PARTS, FOL."

This was Aubrey's first literary work, and was commenced as early as 1656. It was lent, during his life, to many of his learned associates; and the original, which is now in the Ashmolean Museum, has numerous manuscript notes by Evelyn, Ray, Tanner, and Thomas Gale. It was also submitted to the Royal Society in 1675,* and subsequently, when methodized and arranged in its present form, it was dedicated to the Earl of Pembroke, then President of that scientific body. Perhaps in the hope that it would be published by the society, the author made a fair copy of the work, which he presented to them, and which is still preserved in their valuable library.

In 1719 Dr. Rawlinson printed the *Dedication* and *Preface*, as addenda to Aubrey's *History of Surrey* (vol. v. p. 403). These he probably copied from the original. The transcript in the Royal Society's library was quoted by Walpole in the first chapter of his *Anecdotes of Painting* (1762). Gough states that he could not find the work mentioned in Mr. Robertson's catalogue of that library (*British Topography*, vol. ii. p. 515); and he does not appear to have taken the pains to make further search. Warton and Huddesford refer to the original, in the list of Aubrey's manuscripts at Oxford, in a note to the *Life of Anthony à Wood*.

The original manuscript in the Ashmolean Museum consists of two folio volumes, bound in vellum. Its full titles are, " The Natural Historie of Wiltshire," and " Memoires of Naturall Remarques in the county of Wilts; to which are annexed Observables of the same kind in the county of Surrey and Flyntshire. By Mr. John Aubrey, R.S.S." The notes respecting Surrey and Flintshire, if ever written, do not form part of the present manuscript. The title-pages bear the dates 1685 and 1686, when the contents appear to have been arranged and transcribed by the author. It is dedicated to " The Right Honourable Thomas Earle of Pembroke and

---

* The following is part of a letter from Aubrey to Wood, dated, " Twelfe day, 1675. I have written ye *Natural Historie* (for Dr Plotts) *of Wilts* and Surrey, besides pieces of other counties; ten sheetes closely written, and shall send him more. As I was sending it to Oxon our Secretary hearing of it, thought fit the R. Soc. should first be made acquainted with it, which gave them two or three dayes entertainment, wch they were pleased to like." Original, in the *Ballard Collection, ut supra*.

Montgomerie, Lord Herbert of Caerdiffe, one of the Privy Councill to their Majesties, President of the Royall Societie, &c., my singular good Lord."

The history of this manuscript is narrated in the preface, which commences with a kind of apology for the work, as a novelty in literature. In this Aubrey says that, " 'Till about the year 1649, when Experimental Philosophy was first cultivated by a Club at Oxford, it was held a strange Presumption for a man to attempt an Innovation in Learning, and not to be good manners to be more knowing than his Neighbours and Forefathers. I was from my childhood affected with the view of things *rare*, which is the beginning of Philosophy ; and though I have not had leisure to make any considerable proficiency in it, yet I was carried on with a ^secret^strong impulse to undertake this Taske ; I knew not why, unless for my owne private pleasure ; Credit there was none, for it getts the ^contempt^disrespect of a man's neighbours. But I could not rest quiet till I had obeyed this secret call. Mr. Camden, Dr. Plott, and Mr. Wood confess the ^like^same. I am the first that ever made an Essay of this kind for Wiltshire, and (for ought I know) in the nation ; having begun it A° 1656. In the year 1675 I became acquainted with Dr. Robert Plott, who had then his Natural Historie of Oxfordshire upon the Loome, which I seeing he did perform so excellently well, desired him to undertake Wiltshire ; and I would give him all my papers, as I did also my papers of Surrey as to the naturall things, and offer'd my farther assistance. But he was then invited into Stafford-shire, to illustrate that Countie : which having finished in December 1684, I importuned him againe to undertake this county : but he replied, He was so taken up in the Musæum Ashmoleanum, that he should meddle no more in that kind (unlesse it were for his native countie of Kent), and therefore wish'd me to finish and publish what I had begun. Considering therefore that if I should not doe this myselfe, my papers might either perish, or be sold in an auction, and somebody else (as is not uncommon) put his name to my paines ; and not knowing any one that would undertake this Designe while I live ; I have tumultuarily stitch'd up what I have many years since collected, being chiefly but the observation of my frequent road between South and North Wilts (that is, between Broad Chalke and Easton-Piers). If I had had then leisure I would willingly have searched the naturals of the whole County. It is now fifteen yeares since I left this country, and have at this distance inserted such additions as I can call to mind; so that methinks this description is like a picture that Mr. Edwd Bathurst, B.D., of Trin. Coll. Oxon., drew of Dr. Kettle, some yeares after his death, by strength of memory only; he had so strong an Idea of him, and it did well resemble him. I hope hereafter it may be an incitement to some ingeniouse and public-spirited young Wiltshire man, to polish and compleat what I have here delivered rough-hewen, for I have not leasure to heighten my stile."* This is dated "London, Gresham College, June 6, 1685."

The work is divided into chapters, with the following titles: 1. Air.—2. Springs Medicinall.—3. Rivers.—4. Earthes.—5. Minerals.—6. Stones.—7. Formed Stones. —8. A Digression, ad mentem Mr. R. Hook, R.S.S.—9. Plantes (Herbes, Trees). —10. Beastes.—11. Fishes.—12. Birds.—13. Insects and Reptiles.—14. Men and Women.—15. Arts, Inventions.—16. Architecture.—17. Of the Grandure of the Herberts, Earles of Pembroke—Learned men who received pensions from those Earles—Wilton House and Garden.—18. Worthies (Writers and Illustrious Men). —19. Agriculture and Implements.—20. The Downes.—21. Shepherds and Pastoralls.—22. Sheep and Wooll.—23. The History of Cloathing and Cloathiers of Wilts. —24. Faires and Markets, their rise and decay.—25. Prices of Corne.—26. Weights and Measures.—27. Accidents.—28. Observations on some Register Books, as also the Poores Rates and Taxes of the County, ad mentem D^ni W. Petty.—29. Diseases and Cures.—30. Antiquities and Coines.—31. Sports and Races.—32. Things Præturnatural, e. g. Witchcraft, Phantômes, &c.—33. Draughts of the Seats and Prospects.—34. Forests, Parkes, Chaces.—35. Falling of Rents.—36. Number of Attornies every 30 yeares since H. VIII.

Of these subjects, the first 14,—with the 28th and 29th,—are contained in the first volume; the remainder being carried forward to the second, though with a somewhat different arrangement. Thus chapters 25, 26, 30, 32, and 34, are omitted altogether; and the following new chapters are added:—Local Fatality.—Hawkes and Hawking.—Of Gardens (Lavington Garden, Chelsea Garden, &c.)

One of Ray's original letters to Aubrey, approving of the work, is inserted in the first volume. It is the same which contains the gentle reproof of the latter's credu-

---

* Original, in the *Ashmolean Museum.*

lity quoted in page 5, and has been printed in the fifth volume of Aubrey's *History of Surrey*, p. 408.* The remarks of the author are not confined to Wiltshire; but are apparently derived from personal observations made in different counties. A few dried botanical specimens are preserved in the chapter on *Plants*, with Aubrey's notes of their locality and date, and other MS. notes, by Ray. Annexed to the chapter on *Fishes*, and carefully folded up in a small piece of paper, is the " *bone* found in the head of a carp : a good medicine for the apoplectick, or falling sickness." A pamphlet and three Gazettes, containing accounts of different Earthquakes; A manuscript "Explication of the heat of the Waters of Bath," (By Edw. Jorden, of Bath, and Mons. Nich. L'Emery, Chymist,) and a small printed "Treatise on Wool," (a presentation copy to Aubrey from the author, George Clark,) are inserted in appropriate places. There are several memoranda by Aubrey alluding to his gifts of "petrified shells," "naturall iron bullets," &c. to the Royal Society, and to the Ashmolean Museum. In the seventh chapter he mentions "a Turkey stone ring" which he gave to Robert Boyle, Esq., describing the variations of its nebulæ ; under the head of *Men and Women* there are some marvellous stories of longevity, and of monstrous births ; under *Diseases and Cures*, some very absurd prescriptions ; and under *Parish Registers*, several curious extracts from those of Broad Chalk, Wiltshire, " according to the way prescribed by the Honble Sir Wm Petty, Knight." The eighth chapter, which is termed *A Digression*, is " an Hypothesis of the Terrestrial Globe." Ray expressed an unfavourable opinion of this "Digression," which he thought might be very well left out. The following sentences exemplify the writer's notions : " The earth we now do inhabit is rough and uneven, and appears to have been ye ruines of an old one. As the world was torn by earthquakes, as also the vaulture by time foundered and fell in, so the water subsided, and the dry land appear'd. Then why might not that change alter ye center of gravity of ye earth? Before this the pole of the Ecliptick perhaps was the pole of the world. Now (1691) Mr. Edmund Halley, R.S.S. hath an hypothesis that the World is only about 500 miles thick, and that a Terella moves within it, wch causes the variation of the needle : and in the center a Sun." In the same chapter the author says, "On St. Andrew's

---

* Other epistles from Ray respecting this MS. are printed in *Letters from the Bodleian*, vol. ii. p. 158—164.

Day, 1666, my Lord Brouncker, Mr. Wyld, Dr. Charlton, and I, riding in a coach towards Gresham Colledge, (the Anniversary Day,) at ye corner of Holborn Bridge, a cellar of coals was opened by the labourers (who digged ye rubbish and foundations), and there were burning coals (which we saw) which burnt ever since the Great Fire; but being pent so close from air, there was very little waste."* In chap. 17, which illustrates "the grandeur of the Pembroke family," and describes their splendid seat at Wilton, is the following passage; which is here quoted as a matter of curiosity, throwing a doubt (as it does) upon the authorship of one of the most celebrated verses of the seventeenth century.

> " Underneath this sable hearse
> Lies the subject of all verse,
> Sidney's sister—Pembroke's mother.
> Death, ere thou kill'st such another,
> Fair, and wise, and learn'd as she,
> Time will throw a dart at thee."

" These verses were made by Mr. *Williā* Browne who wrote the *Pastoralls*, and they are inserted there."

The above lines are almost universally attributed to Ben Jonson : it is therefore essential to observe that Aubrey is not alone in stating them to be by Browne, the author of the *Pastorals;* for, in his note upon the subject, he left a blank for the latter's Christian name, " William ; " which was filled up by Evelyn when he perused the manuscript. Indeed, Evelyn not only filled up such blank, but added, as a further note, " *William*, Governor to ye now E. of Oxford."

As " Advice to the Painter or Graver," there is, at the end of the work, a list of the illustrations Aubrey appears to have thought most desirable. Besides his own portrait after Loggan, he proposed to have a " Mappe" of Salisbury, with exterior and interior views of the Cathedral ; Views of Malmesbury Abbey Church ; " Priory St. Maries, juxta Kington St. Michael ; " and, among " Houses of lesser note," " The Mannour-house of Kington St. Michael." Amongst the *prospects*, he desired to have one " from the Garret at Easton-Piers, South-east, a delicate prospect." " If these views," he says, " were well donn, they would make a glorious Volume by itselfe,

---

* This memorable conflagration continued from the 2nd to the 6th of September. St. Andrew's Day is the 30th of November.

and like enough it might take well in the World. It were an inconsiderable charge to these Persons of Qualitie: and it would remaine to Posterity, when their Families are gonn, and their Buildings ruin'd by time, or Fire, as we have seen that stupendous Fabrick of Paul's Church, not a stone left on a stone, and lives now onely in Mr Hollar's Etchings in Sr William Dugdale's History of Paul's. I am not displeased with this Thought as a Desideratum, but I doe never expect to see it donn: so few men have the hearts to doe publique good: to give 3, 4, or 5li. for a Copper Plate." There are about three hundred pages in the first volume, and three hundred and twenty in the second.

The Royal Society's copy of the " Natural History of Wiltshire" appears to be a close transcript of the original. The two parts are bound as one volume; and there is inserted, at p. 260, a MS. copy of a " Survey of our Lady Church at Salisbury taken by Dr Christopher Wren (since Sir Christopher), Anno Domini, 1669, being invited down to do it by Seth Ward, Lord Bishop of Sarum." Mr. Halliwell, in his " Catalogue of the Miscellaneous MSS. in the Library of the Royal Society," (8vo. 1840,) states that " this work is in course of publication, under the able editorship of Sir Thomas Phillipps, Bart.," thus committing the error of previous writers, by confounding the manuscript now referred to with the *Description of North Wiltshire*, already noticed.

It is hoped and expected that the WILTSHIRE TOPOGRAPHICAL SOCIETY will publish the " Natural History," as a companion to the present memoir.

IV. " PERAMBULATION OF HALFE THE COUNTY OF SURREY, FOL." [*In the Ashmolean Museum.*]

THE circumstances attending the production of Aubrey's *Perambulation*, or *History of Surrey*, have been already mentioned, (vide pp. 49, 64,) and the work itself, as printed under the care of Dr. Rawlinson, in five vols. 8vo., 1719, though now scarce, is in many public and private libraries.

The manuscript in the Ashmolean Museum does not appear to contain the whole of the work, but comprises about one hundred and eighty leaves of paper, (foolscap folio, stitched,) written on one side only, with occasional corrections on the opposite pages. It contains many notes by Evelyn, and the original of his letter to Aubrey, which is given in the printed work. There is also a dedication to "the Honourable and Vertuous Charles Howard of Norfolk, and the Honoured and Vertuous John Evelyn, of Deptford, Esquire," also many slight drawings, by the author, of the principal seats in the county, armorial bearings, &c. In Manning and Bray's *History of Surrey*, vol. iii. p. 685, Aubrey's perambulation is spoken of with respect. The authors state that, " by his labours, many monumental inscriptions have been preserved, which have since been destroyed. Although his copies are by no means exact as to spelling, his dates are seldom found to be incorrect."

In Gough's *British Topography*, (vol. ii. p. 262,) Granger is quoted, to the effect that another edition of the *History of Surrey* was published in 1723; and Worrall, in *Bibliotheca Topographica Anglicana*, mentions an edition in 1723, with *only a new title*. In Lowndes's *Bibliographer's Manual* copies of the work are said to have realized the following prices: " Sotheby, Morocco, £7. 12s. 6d., Sir P. Thompson £9. 16s. 6d., Dent, Russia, £19. 5s. 0d., Towneley, Russia, £26. 5s. 0d., Nassau £26. 15s. 6d., Beckford, 1817, Morocco, £29. 8s. 0d." According to Worrall it was published at £1 5s. 0d.

V. " MISCELLANEA, FOL."

THIS manuscript is not in the Ashmolean Museum, nor am I able to give any account of it. It may be supposed to have contained materials for Aubrey's *Miscellanies*, which will be noticed in a future page.

VI. " LIVES, 3 PARTS. . . . .)
VII. Mr TH. HOBBES' LIFE IN ENGLISH."}

THESE are the works by which Aubrey is best known to the public: a full account of the circumstances under which they were written has been already given. It is evident on comparing these manuscripts with Wood's *Athenæ Oxonienses* that several of the lives printed in the latter were compiled from materials collected by Aubrey; but Wood made many additions and corrections to them, as may be seen by collating his notice of James Harrington with that written by Aubrey, and printed ante, p. 35—37.

Neither Rawlinson nor Gough, in their remarks respecting Aubrey, took any notice of the *Lives.* It is said that Granger, in his *Biographical History of England,* (1769), acknowledged his obligations to them for several anecdotes; and that Lysons used them in his *Environs of London,* (1791).*

The Aubrey manuscripts, and especially the *Lives of Eminent Men,* attracted a great degree of attention from some of the most eminent literati towards the latter part of the last century, and led indeed to controversy and differences of opinion, the history of which would form a curious chapter in the literary annals of the country.

Thomas Warton, the historian of English poetry, as a Fellow of Trinity College, Oxford, and a true lover of antiquities, devoted much of his time and attention to the preparation of the *Life and Literary Remains of Ralph Bathurst, D.D.*, which he published in one volume 8vo., in 1761. Bathurst had been a contemporary and intimate friend of Aubrey, and was President of the college to which they both belonged, from 1664 to 1704.

From the *Memoir of Aubrey* by *Dr. Rawlinson,* from Hearne's edition of *Anthony à Wood's Life,* and from the *Biographia Britannica,* Warton necessarily derived a general knowledge of the talents and the labours of Aubrey; and in the pursuit of inquiries for his *Memoir of Bathurst,* the *Ashmoleam Museum* afforded him an obvious source for material information and assistance. There he consulted with great advantage the manuscript collections so often referred to. In the preface to his memoir, after adverting to other libraries whence he had obtained aid, Warton remarks, " But I found much greater assistance from Aubrey's Collection of Letters, in the Ashmolean Museum, containing a correspondence between the most learned of Dr. Bathurst's contemporaries." Those letters (respecting which see Article XIX. p. 118) are repeatedly quoted by Warton, who also refers, in this volume, to other portions of the manuscripts. Amongst these, Aubrey's notices of *Bathurst,* and

* See Caulfield's *Inquiry into the conduct of Malone,*—a pamphlet fully noticed hereafter, p. 103.

his memoir of *Dr. Kettle*, also a president of Trinity College, necessarily called for special notice from the biographer of the former. The *Life of Hobbes*, too, as containing anecdotes of Bathurst, is alluded to; and the *Lives*, generally, are described by Warton (p. 153, note) as "An account of English Writers, especially our Poets, with many of whom Aubrey was intimately acquainted, containing several new and curious anecdotes of their lives." He proceeds to state, from personal examination of the work, that it was lent by the author to Anthony à Wood, whose obligations to it he describes, adding the Lives of Spenser and of Shakspere, "as a specimen" of the manuscript. A letter from Bathurst to Aubrey, commending his *Monumenta Britannica*, induces Warton to advert to that work; of which, however, it appears his only knowledge was derived from the printed account by Dr. Rawlinson. It may be observed that Warton refers to the papers with scrupulous minuteness; for instance, "Aubrey's MSS. Lives, Mus. Ashmol. Part I, No. 10, folio, p. 36, Cod. Ashmol." "Collection of Original Letters, MSS. Mus. Ashmol. No. 15, folio. In Ashmole's Study, vol. i." &c.

In 1780, Warton published a *Life of Sir Thomas Pope*, the founder of Trinity College (8vo.), wherein he again refers, incidentally, to the *Lives*, and especially to that of Dr. Kettle. At page 185, he gives quotations from "Sir Thomas Pope's breviary—written and illuminated—given by John Aubrey, the antiquarian, to the Ashmolean Museum." (vide the present Memoir, ante, p. 83). He adds, on the authority of a "Letter to Wood," in the *Ballard volume* already frequently quoted in this memoir, that "Aubrey had intended to place this breviary in its proper repository, Trinity College Library; but, having conceived some prejudice against Dr. Bathurst, the president, he changed his design, and gave it to the Ashmolean Museum."

In conjunction with William Huddesford, also a Fellow of Trinity College, and then keeper of the Ashmolean Museum, Warton published, in 1772, a new edition of *Anthony à Wood's* Life, together with *Memoirs of Leland and Hearne*; and, in a note to the first of these, they appended a list of Aubrey's manuscripts in the museum; but it is remarkable that they entirely omitted to notice in that list the *Lives of Eminent Men*.

Dr. Farmer, in his *Essay on the Learning of Shakespeare* (8vo. 1767), thus mentions Aubrey's *Lives:* "The celebrated Mr Warton in his Life of Dr Bathurst hath favoured us with some hearsay particulars concerning Shakespeare, from a MS. of Aubrey's which had been in the hands of Wood, and I ought not to suppress them, as the last seems to make against my doctrine.* They came originally, I find, on consulting the MS., from one Mr Beeston,† and I am sure Mr Warton, whom I have the honour to call my friend, will be in no pain about their credit." (p. 36) Farmer then quotes Aubrey's notice of Shakspere, and partially refutes it; adding, "It is therefore sufficiently clear that poor Antony à Wood had too much reason for his character of Aubrey."

The biographical writings of Aubrey in the next place attracted the attention of Malone; who, in the course of his task as an editor and commentator on Shakspere, derived much curious information from the papers of the old topographer and antiquary. Some passages in the *first part* of vol. i. of Malone's edition of *Shakspeare* (8vo. 1790),‡ shew that when that was printed his knowledge of the Aubrey manuscripts was limited to the facts previously made public; but it is evident that, before issuing the *second part* of the same volume, he had made some immediate use of the originals; though still (there is reason to believe) not from personal examination, but merely by extracts, furnished by Warton, with whom he was on friendly terms. "Since my remarks," says Malone, "on the epitaph said to have been made by Shakspeare on John O'Combe, were printed, it occurred to me that the manuscript papers of Mr. Aubrey, preserved in the Ashmolean Museum at Oxford, might throw some light on that subject."§ He then gives a short but circumstantial account of Aubrey's life and writings; together with the favourable opinions of his literary merits, which have been quoted in p. 6 of the preceding Memoir. He proceeds as follows:—"The anecdotes concerning D'Avenant, in Wood's *Athenæ*

---

* Farmer's theory was that Shakspere did not receive the advantages of a classical education.

† This is an error on the part of Farmer. Aubrey derived certain information respecting *Spenser* (not Shakspere), from Mr. Beeston.

‡ *Notes to Rowe's Life* in Malone's *Shakspeare*, vol. i. part i. pp. 160, 164.

§ *Historical Account of the English Stage*, in Malone's *Shakspeare*, vol. i. part ii. p. 166.

Oxonicnscs, were, like the copious and accurate account of Milton, transcribed lite-rally from Aubrey's papers. What has been there suggested [that D'Avenant was Shakspere's son] is confirmed by a subsequent passage in the MS., which has been imperfectly obliterated, and which Wood did not print; though, in one of his own unpublished manuscripts, now in the Bodleian Library, he has himself told the same story. The line which is imperfectly obliterated, in a different ink, and therefore probably by another hand than that of Aubrey, tells us (as Mr. Warton, who has been able to trace the words through the obliteration, informs me) that D'Avenant was Shakspeare's son." Malone, a few pages onward, prints what he calls "an exact transcript of the whole article [by Aubrey] relating to Shakspeare, from the original;" and this, which is given more accurately than it had previously been by Warton and Farmer, is accompanied by nine pages of critical commentary upon Aubrey's anecdotes. Indeed, it is evident that this editor of Shakspere fairly and fully appreciated Aubrey's industry and his accuracy of record.

In page 269, Malone makes the following additional remarks respecting D'Avenant:—" I have mentioned in a preceding page," he says, " that the account given of him by Wood was taken from Mr. Aubrey's MS. Since that sheet was printed Mr. Warton has obligingly furnished me with an exact transcript of the article relating to D'Avenant,* which, as it contains some particulars not noticed by Wood, I shall here subjoin." Yet it is remarkable that in the transcript which follows, the *" imperfectly obliterated"* passages, so ingeniously observed by Warton, are not given.

Soon after the appearance of Malone's edition of Shakspere the literary world was agitated by the famous discussion respecting the *Ireland forgeries ;*† and this led to

---

* There is no doubt that the " exact transcript" of the memoir of Shakspere, previously given by Malone, was also supplied by his friend Warton. Mr. Charles Knight, in his recent *Biography* of Shakspere, notices the traditional account of him by Aubrey, and endeavours to reconcile some of its statements with the few facts which have been satisfactorily ascertained.

† The original documents prepared by William Henry Ireland, junior, and promulgated with so much temporary success, together with his own manuscript " Confession" of the whole course of his deceptions, are in the possession of Lewis Pocock, Esquire, F.S.A. London.

Malone's able " *Inquiry into the authenticity of certain papers and instruments attributed to Shakspeare,*" which was printed in 8vo. in 1796. By this we find that subsequently to the publication of his " *Shakspeare,*" Malone had examined Aubrey's manuscripts, which appear to have been previously known to him only through other sources. In page 200, he says, " Of the whole of Aubrey's biographical collections, deposited in the Ashmolean Museum, I made a transcript last summer, which will hereafter be laid before the publick ;" and in an appendix, he quotes, " from a paper entitled *Nouvelles,** MS. Aubrey in Mus. Ashmol.," a short notice of the Penny Post, and an account of the "Bank of Credit at Devonshire House, Bishopsgate Street." The last was projected in the seventeenth century, and, though unsuccessful, led, about eleven years afterwards, to the establishment of the Bank of England.

Further proof that Malone made extracts personally from the Aubrey papers about this period is afforded by a pamphlet written by James Caulfield, a London print-seller, who had been attracted to the same curious materials with a view to pecuniary profit. Caulfield's pamphlet likewise appeared in 1796, and was called " *An Inquiry into the conduct of Edmond Malone, Esq., concerning the Manuscript papers of John Aubrey, F.R.S., in the Ashmolean Museum, Oxford.* London: Printed for J. Caulfield, No. 11, Old Compton-street, Soho." 8vo. pp. 19. The author, who produced some volumes of curious biographies, with portraits, states that about the year 1788 his attention was directed to the manuscript of the *Lives of Eminent Men*, which he intended to have printed ; but he did not examine it personally till 1796, when, by the permission of Charles Lloyd, Esq. then Keeper of the Ashmolean Museum, he copied some of the memoirs. After his return to London, Caulfield " wrote to Oxford to obtain a copy of the fine Drawing by Faithorne of John Aubrey, which he proposed to prefix to the work. But in the course of Engraving this portrait, he understood Mr Malone was occupied on the same plan with himself." He accordingly had an interview with him, wherein, as is evident from Caulfield's narrative, much jealously was mutually shown ; and, having failed to effect any compromise with Malone, by

---

* This is not in the Ashmolean Museum. It will be seen that a chapter of Aubrey's *Monumenta Britannica* bore the title of *Nouvelles.*

which either party should abandon his project, the speculating bookseller "indus-
triously applied himself to the work, and made a contract with an able artist, to
furnish him with a considerable quantity of drawings; which he gave into the hands
of celebrated Engravers. These plates on an average could not be finished under
twelve guineas each." When five of them were completed, Caulfield learnt that
Malone was endeavouring to do him "an irreparable injury, by using his interest at
Oxford to stop his pursuit in gaining the manuscript complete: consequently to
leave him at a considerable expence, in the midst of a heavy undertaking."* His
intended publication was, notwithstanding, announced to appear in quarto numbers,
with the title of "The Oxford Cabinet, or Aubrean Miscellany;" but on going once
more to Oxford, before any portion of it was published, he was informed, "to his
inexpressible surprise, that, in consequence of a letter from Mr Malone to the Keeper,
the MSS. were no longer to be consulted; particularly however excluding him: and
the only answer he could obtain from Mr Lake, the deputy keeper, was they were
carefully locked up, and no longer in his power to shew to any person whatever."
Upon this Caulfield immediately wrote to Malone, complaining of the injury
inflicted on him, inquiring his motive for doing him "so wilful a prejudice," and
threatening to publish a statement of the facts. "To this letter Mr Malone sent a
verbal message down by his servant, stating that it required no answer;" whereupon
the *Inquiry* was printed. Caulfield indignantly disputes the right of Malone to the
exclusive use of Aubrey's papers; shows that he was not the *first* who had referred
to them for literary purposes; and incidentally states that "Mr Seward had contemplated using them, but, out of courtesy to Malone, with whom he was personally
intimate, had relinquished such intention." He complains that his rival had great
facilities afforded him, the papers being "removed to his house from the museum;"

---

* Shortly before this Caulfield had again seen the manuscript, and observed, on the wrapper of the second
part, the following inscription, in Malone's hand-writing: " These fragments collected and arranged by E. M.
1792." The *fragments* in question are the remnants of the volume which (so greatly to the vexation of
Aubrey) was mutilated by Anthony à Wood: they remain as they were arranged by Malone. Now the above
inscription shows that the latter had seen the manuscript four years prior to Caulfield, who took pains to
show that he had contemplated printing it as early as 1788.

and finally makes a severe allusion to Malone's "big, bloated pride," and challenges a contradiction to his statements.

Malone, however, seems to have treated with silent contempt the complaints and threatenings of Caulfield, who, acting upon his engagement to proceed with such materials as he possessed, published the first part of his work, with the following full title : "The Oxford Cabinet; consisting of Engravings from Original Pictures in the Ashmolean Museum, and other public and private collections; with Biographical Anecdotes, by John Aubrey, F.R.S. and other celebrated writers. London. Printed for James Caulfield, William Street, Adelphi, 1797." Of the six numbers promised, only two were published. These contain ten of Aubrey's biographical notices, including that of his ancestor, Dr. William Aubrey, which is accompanied by a portrait of him; also others of John Aubrey, and of the Tradescant family, &c.; making in all nine prints, and a few woodcuts. The book has neither preface nor introduction : it is very scarce, as is also the *Inquiry*, above quoted; but copies of each may be consulted in the Royal Library of the British Museum. They were both very unfavorably criticised in the *Gentleman's Magazine*, for 1797-8.

Aubrey is again referred to by Malone in his edition of Dryden's *Miscellaneous Prose Works* (4 vols. 8vo., 1800). He states that Dryden's "Eleanora, a Panegyrical Poem," (published in 1692,) was written, as may be inferred from its dedication, at the request of the first Earl of Abingdon, in praise of his deceased Countess, granddaughter of Sir John Danvers, the regicide. "It is a singular circumstance," says Malone, "that our author should have written this poem at the desire of a nobleman with whom he was not personally acquainted, in praise of a lady whom he never saw. This however was evidently a task undertaken for a pecuniary reward; and the *commission* perhaps was procured by Mr. Aubrey, a common friend of our author and the Earl of Abingdon." * He does not appear to have been aware that Aubrey was related to the family of Danvers.

Until his death, in 1812, Malone continued actively employed in collecting materials for the illustration of Shakspere; and with that view he employed

* Dryden's *Miscellaneous Prose Works* by Malone, vol. iv. p. 57.

Bartolozzi, as already mentioned, to engrave the portrait of John Aubrey, whose writings the commentator evidently held in high esteem. His collections were arranged by his executor and friend James Boswell, for the edition of Shakspere, published in 1822, in 21 volumes, 8vo. Most of the remarks given by Malone in his own edition, on topics connected with the names of Shakspere, D'Avenant, and Aubrey, were repeated in that of Boswell, though his improved arrangement of the matter led to their transposition in various ways. Malone's assumption that John Shakspere, the poet's father, was a glover, had led him, after publishing his previous remarks, to a further examination of the *Lives of Eminent Men*, and to the following judicious remarks on the value of Aubrey's testimony : " If the representation attempted to be given of this ingenious and unfortunate gentleman were just and well founded ; if it were true that every one who is weak in one place must necessarily be weak in all ; that all those persons who in the last century were idle enough to put their faith in judicial astrology, and to give credit to stories of preternatural appearances of the dead, were fools ; and their judgment or testimony of no value on any subject whatever, however unconnected with these weaknesses ; then, in this large list of *ninnies*, must we class, with Mr. Aubrey, the accomplished and literate Charles the First ; the grave and judicious Clarendon ; the witty Duke of Buckingham ; the fertile and ingenious Dryden ; and many other names of equal celebrity :—they must all ' bench by his side,' and must be set down as persons not capable of forming a true judgment on any matter whatsoever presented to them, and wholly unworthy of credit." * In the third volume of Boswell's edition (p. 278) Aubrey's account of D'Avenant is repeated ; and there the " imperfectly obliterated" line, which had been traced by Warton more than twenty years before, was for the first time made public. It runs thus,—" Now by the way his mother had a very light report. In those days she was called a trader." There is also the following passage which Malone has not printed in his own edition :—" I have heard Parson Robert [D'Avenant's brother] say that Mr. William Shakespeare has given him a hundred kisses." It is remarkable that these particular erasures (for both passages are struck through with a pen in the original)

* Boswell's edition of *Shakspeare*, vol. ii. p. 70.

have very recently attracted the attention of Mr. J. O. Halliwell; who, not being aware of the notice they had received from Warton and Malone, has recorded the omitted words as new and interesting contributions to the history of Shakspere, "which had hitherto escaped the researches of all the biographers of our great dramatist." "During a recent visit to Oxford," he says, " I had the curiosity to inspect the original manuscript, and found that two paragraphs, *scratched* through, but not with a contemporary pen, had escaped notice. By the aid of a strong light, and a powerful magnifying glass, I was enabled to read them entirely, with the exception of a few letters." Mr. Halliwell's version is not literally the same as Malone's; but he states that " Mr. Kirtland, Assistant Keeper of the Ashmolean Museum, who is deeply skilled in palæography, agreed with me in my reading of the blotted passages." *

In 1813 nearly the whole of Aubrey's *Lives of Eminent Men* were published in a very amusing and interesting work edited by the Rev. Dr. Bliss and the late Rev. J. Walker, of Oxford. This was originally intended to consist chiefly of letters by distinguished literary men of the seventeenth century, preserved in the Bodleian Library; whence it is familiarly known as *Letters from the Bodleian* (paged as 2, but bound in 3 vols. 8vo., see ante, p. 2). It contains one hundred and sixty-two letters from that extensive library, with the following appendices: No. 1. Eight Letters from the Ashmolean Museum (six of which were addressed to Aubrey) ; Nos. 2 and 3. Accounts of Hearne's Journies to Whaddon Hall and to Reading, from his MS. Diaries; No. 4. The *Lives of Eminent Men*, by John Aubrey; and No. 5. His *Life of Thomas Hobbes*. One hundred and thirty of Aubrey's *Lives* are thus printed; and the appendix No. 4. consequently embraces one-half of the work. In their preface the editors say, " The object has been to give these Lives verbatim, without correction or addition. That they possess a claim to the title of *literary curiosities*, will readily be allowed, since there is scarcely a Life without some anecdote hitherto unpublished; and the author's description of the personal

* Halliwell's *Essay on the Character of Sir John Falstaff, as originally exhibited by Shakespeare, in the two parts of King Henry IV.* 12mo. 1841, pp. 47—50.

appearance, and domestic habits, of most of the individuals of whom he writes, is singularly interesting."

William Godwin published in 1815 a quarto volume of the *Lives of Edward and John Phillips, Nephews and Pupils of Milton*, wherein he gives entire Aubrey's account of Milton, from these *Lives*, admitting it to be "undoubtedly of considerable value and authenticity," but at the same time remarking that it is, "to a certain degree, stamped with the coldness of a by-stander or clerk of the court," whilst the memoir of the poet by Edward Phillips is "a monument of sober affection and veneration." This is perhaps hardly just to the merits of the article referred to; the accuracy of which received a singular confirmation in 1823. In that year the late Robert Lemon, the Deputy-Keeper of the State-Paper Office, discovered in that establishment the manuscript of a work by Milton, before unknown, except from a notice of it by Aubrey, who described it as "Idea Theologiæ, in manuscript, in the hands of Mr. Skinner, a merchant's sonne, in Mark Lane." There are papers in the same office tending to show that it passed there directly from Daniel Skinner, the person alluded to by Aubrey; in consequence of prohibition, on the part of the Government of 1676, against its being published. A full analysis of the manuscript, with its history, and Aubrey's statements on the subject, will be found in Todd's edition of Milton's *Poetical Works*, 8vo., vol. i. p. 184, 1842.*

Aubrey's account of Ben Jonson has been much underrated by Gifford, in his biographical notice of that poet. The latter says, that "whoever expects a rational account of any fact, however trite, from Aubrey, will meet with disappointment. . . . In short, Aubrey thought little, believed much, and confused everything."† Aubrey's statement that Jonson was tutor to Sir Walter Raleigh's son, was disputed by Gifford, but has been confirmed, by the complete copy of Jonson's *Conversations*:‡ and, although the antiquary's assertion (on the authority of Sir Ed-

---

* Bishop Burgess read an elaborate and learned paper on the subject before the Royal Society of Literature.

† *The Works of Ben Jonson; with Notes, and a Biographical Memoir*, by W. Gifford. (9 vols. 8vo. 1816.) Vol. i. p. xix.

‡ Published in 1842 by the *Shakspere Society*, under the Editorship of David Laing, Esq.

ward Sherburne) that the poet "killed Mr. Marlow, on Bun-hill, comeing from the Green Curtain play-house," is incorrect; yet it has been ascertained by Mr. Collier, that Ben Jonson really killed Gabriel Spencer, the player, in a duel in a field, near Hoxton;—a fact which probably led to the erroneous information given to Aubrey. Indeed there is generally a great deal of truth in everything the latter says; and there can be no doubt that as our knowledge of the matters he alludes to is extended, many of his statements, which now appear to rest on slight or insufficient grounds, will be corroborated.

Gifford further says, " Aubrey's authority is seldom to be relied on; a greater blunderer never existed; as Wood himself discovered when too late: he calls him a ' roving, maggotty-pated man,' and such he truly was."

Those who have perused Gifford's *Auto-biography*, in his translation of Juvenal's Satires, would expect more liberality of sentiment and courtesy of language than are to be found in these harsh and overbearing comments on Aubrey; but, from the long continued exercise of the critical pen in the prejudiced career of political and religious partizanship, the writer's mind became callous and intolerant. Besides, it is quite evident that Gifford had not examined the valuable manuscript collections of Aubrey. Every discriminating reader of the foregoing pages will be enabled to appreciate the injustice of the language used by the editor of Jonson's works.

With respect to Aubrey's memoirs generally, it is unnecessary to use the language of commendation, as the important addition which they form to our knowledge of the persons and events referred to is already fully acknowledged. The care taken by the author to ensure accuracy in his statements, and to record the names of his informants, in all cases where he does not speak from his own knowledge, stamp them with a high degree of authenticity.

Among the most curious and interesting memoirs may be particularized the notices of the author's ancestor, Dr. William Aubrey; of Dr. Kettle, Oughtred, Sir William D'Avenant, Lord Bacon, Sir John Denham (with whom he was very intimate), Sir Kenelm Digby and Lady Venetia Stanley, Sir John Suckling, Dr. Wallis, Francis Potter, Selden, General Monk, Ben Jonson, Milton, and, notwithstanding its supposed inaccuracies, Shakspere.

The original manuscript of the *Lives of Eminent Men* consists of three parts, foolscap folio. The second (mutilated by Wood, and arranged by Malone,) has about twenty leaves only, whereas the others are of considerable bulk. There are indexes by Aubrey to the first and third parts, and there appears to be several lives not yet published, though they are certainly of minor character. The desultory manner in which Aubrey put his materials together is shown by inter-lineations, corrections, and additions, in almost every page of the manuscript.

The *Life of Hobbes,* which is a separate manuscript, has been fully mentioned in a previous page, 54. It formed the Appendix No. 5 to the *Letters from the Bodleian,* and is there very accurately given from the original. It is a valuable memoir, and is repeatedly quoted with commendation by D'Israeli in his *Quarrels of Authors,* vol. iii.

VIII. " AN APPARATUS OF THE LIVES OF ENGLISH MATHEMATICIANS. A Q^r AT GRESHAM COLLEDGE." [*In the Ashmolean Museum.*]

THESE lives occupy sixteen leaves, foolscap folio, written on one side only, and paged by the author. They are stitched together, and fastened inside the cover of part iii. of the *Lives of Eminent Men,* with the following title: "An Apparatus for the Lives of our English Mathematical Writers. By M^r Jo. Aubrey, R.S.S. March 25th, 1690." Two printed books on arithmetic (of about the reign of Henry VIII.,) are noticed in this manuscript; which contains memoranda for the Lives of Dr. Record, James Peele, Leonard Digges, Thomas Digges, Cyprian Lucar, Edmund Gunter, Richard Norwood, John Wells, Thomas Merry, Edward Wright, Henry Coley, and Thomas Streete.

IX. "IDEA OF EDUCATION OF YOUNG GENTLEMEN FROM 9 TO 18, FOL. THE CORRECT COPIE IS W^th ANTHONY HENLEY, Esqr AT Y^e GRANGE IN HAMP-SHIRE." [*In the Ashmolean Museum.*]

THIS manuscript was correctly mentioned by Warton and Huddesford as an *Idea of Education of Young Gentlemen;* but it is most inaccurately named by Chalmers, in his *Biographical Dictionary*, as *The Idea of Universal Education*. Theories were frequently termed *Ideas* in Aubrey's time :—witness Milton's manuscript *Idea Theologiæ*, mentioned in a former page; Pell's *Idea of Mathematicks;* Templer's *Idea Theologiæ Leviathanis;* and Mackenzie's *Idea Eloquentiæ;* all written about the same era. Hitherto the only published notice of Aubrey's *Idea of Education* was a letter from the Rev. Andrew Paschal to Aubrey, penned after perusing the manuscript, and offering some suggestions for its improvement.*

The preceding pages show the value which the writer himself attached to this production. It comprises about one hundred leaves, foolscap folio, written, on one side only, in a loose and confused manner, and is called on the title-page, "A Private Essay only." It is dated 1683-4, and is an elaborate plan for the formation of schools, or establishments, in which the "Education of Young Gentlemen" should be better conducted, and more independently of the priesthood, than in any academy or college then extant.

In a copy of a letter from Aubrey to Anthony Henley, Esq. written in 1693-4, and annexed to the manuscript, he says, "The Earle of Pembroke hath read it over, and excerpted some things. He approves of it, but is not active. I wish I may live to transcribe a fair copie, from which others may be transcribed. I have some hopes that the Marquis of Worcester may propagate this designe in Wales. It would be but, as it were, saying *fiat*, to yᵉ E. of Pembroke, Lord Worcester, and Lord Ashley, to have it established at Cranburn. But God's will be done. If the nobless have a mind to have their children be put into the Clergie's pockets, much good may it do 'em." He begs that the manuscript (which accompanied the letter) might be returned to him, or to Mr. Hooke at Gresham College, in the event of his decease; and adds, "But I foresee that it will lie there coffined up, and nobody have that generosity to set afloat this noble designe."

The essay is divided into thirty-two chapters, of which the principal are entitled, the Proem; the Institution; Grammar; Mathematicall Prudence; Geometrie; Ethics; Logic; Rhetorique; Civil Law; Method; the Schooles; the Classes; Exercise, in

---

* Aubrey's *History of Surrey*, vol. i. p. xiv.

schoole and for holydayes; the Diet-hall, and Portico; Penances, or Punishments; Orders, or Statutes; Religion, &c.

Under these various heads Aubrey describes the course of study which he considered most desirable in each successive year, for pupils between the ages of nine and eighteen. Speaking of his proposed library, he devotes ten pages to a list of books, which he regarded as best calulated for the instruction of youth; and this is interesting as showing his opinions of the classics, and of certain contemporary writers.* He strongly urges instruction in arithmetic of the most useful kind, by means of counters; and recommends that the walls of the class-rooms should be ornamented with portraits of illustrious men, and with emblems and mottoes inculcating practical wisdom and morality. He further advises that the Provost and *Informations* (as he calls the tutors) should be unmarried, and that " Swiss, Dutch, and Scotch men, of good presence, be engaged to teach;" not forgetting " a lusty young Swiss with a long sword,—one that can speak Latin,—to be the porter." His plan makes ample provision for the exercise and amusement of the scholars, who, besides having " 10 or 12 Swiss boys to play with them," were to be taught riding, and out-of-door exercise by a Swiss, and dancing by a Frenchman. The rules for diet are judicious, as well as his reproval of corporal punishment. " I would have no such thing as the turning up of bare buttocks," but on the contrary he advises finger-stocks, and deprivation of amusement, for boys who misconduct themselves. He recommends the study of astrology as " the best guide to direct us to what professions or callings children are by nature most fit or most inclined to." The Essay thus characteristically concludes: " But now (methinkes) I see a black squadron, led up by a crosier staffe (Dr Jo. Fell, Bp. of Oxford), marching from Oxford, to discomfite this pretty Little Flock, and so this my pleasing Dream is at an End. Soli Deo Gloria."

Amongst the places where the author proposed to establish his schools were, Canonbury, Islington; Merton, in Wiltshire; and Cranburne, in Dorsetshire.

---

* In the Ashmolean Museum is a volume containing nine printed pamphlets (small 4to.) thus marked by Aubrey:—" This collection of Gramaticall Learning, and another in 8vo., is in relation to my Idea of the Education of the Noblesse."

X. "Remaines of Gentilisme, 3 parts, sc., about 3 qᵣˢ. With Dʳ Kennet."
[*In the British Museum, being part of the Lansdowne MS. No. 231.*]

THE Lansdowne MS. No. 231, is entitled in the catalogue of that series, "A Volume of Miscellaneous Collections formerly in the possession of Bishop Kennett, but not made by himself." Aubrey's is the third manuscript in the volume, and extends from p. 101 to p. 241. The above note shows that this work was in the possession of Bishop Kennett in 1692 : and after his death it passed, together with his other papers, into the custody of the first Marquess of Lansdowne, whose valuable collection was purchased for the British Museum in 1807. *

This manuscript, which is dated 1688,† has the following title and dedication :—
" Remaines of Gentilisme and Judaisme. By J. Aubrey, R.S.S. To His ever honoured Friend Edmund Wyld,‡ of Geasly Hall, in the County of Salop, Esqʳ, these Remaines of Gentilisme and Judaisme are dedicated, as a small token of ancient Friendship, by his affectionate and humble Servant, J. Aubrey."

A volume of " Anecdotes and Traditions" was edited, in 1839, by W. J. Thoms,

---

* William, Marquess of Lansdowne, whose country seat was Bowood, Wiltshire, about six miles from the birth-place of Aubrey, was not more famed in the political than in the literary and scientific world. His seat was a sort of English Tusculum, where the most distinguished statesmen, artists, literati, and men of science often associated to enjoy " the feast of reason and the flow of soul ;" where the state of nations, of parties, of novelties in literature and art, were discussed and reviewed ; where the obstinacy of a monarch, and the reckless tyranny of a minister, were brought under the severe and condemnatory scrutiny of some of the most potent critics of the age. It would not be a difficult task to trace some of the famed letters of *Junius* to this fountain head (vide Life of Charles Butler, by Dr. Bowring). The value and importance of that portion of the contents of the British Museum, properly called the *Lansdowne Manuscripts*, cannot fail to dignify the character of the illustrious nobleman who amassed and preserved it.

† " London, Sᵗ Bartholomew's Close, Octob. Novemb. Decemb. 1688."

‡ This Mr. Wyld is mentioned by Roger North in his account of the learned associates of the Lord Keeper Guildford : " One Mʳ Wyld, a rich philosopher, lived in Bloomsbury. He was single, and his house a sort of knick-knack-atory. Most of the ingenious persons about town visited him, and among the rest his lordship did suit and service there. This gentleman was of a superior order, and valued himself upon new inventions of his own. He sowed salads in the morning, to be cut for dinner ; and claimed the invention of painted curtains, in varnish, upon silk ; which would bend and not crack ; and his house was furnished with them : and he delighted in nothing more than in shewing his multifarious contrivances." North's *Life of Guildford* (edition 1826), vol. ii. p. 180.

Esq. and published by the Camden Society, the second part of which, as the editor
states in the preface, "is derived from the Lansdowne MS. No. 231, written by the
well-known John Aubrey, and containing his materials (with some subsequent additions by Dr White Kennett, Bishop of Peterborough,) for a work, the publication of
which he had contemplated under the title of 'Remains of Gentilism and Judaism,'
and in which, it appears, he had proposed to draw a parallel between the superstitions of Greece and Rome and those of his own country; finding the records, or
rather traces, of the former, in the works of their Poets, and collecting his English
stores from the communications of his friends. Many interesting passages of this
manuscript have been already transferred by Sir Henry Ellis to his edition of
Brand's *Popular Antiquities*; these with one exception, that of the Funeral Dirge,
have been omitted in the present work; but, combined with those here printed, may
be said to comprise everything deserving of publication contained in the volume."

The specimens selected by Mr. Thoms consist of about seventy short passages,
each of which is illustrated and explained by means of appropriate notes. The
original essay comprises an interesting series of memorials of customs and observances
prevalent in Wiltshire, and other parts of England, in Aubrey's time; but, as the
original is readily accessible in the National Library, it is unnecessary to enlarge
upon its contents.

XI. "VILLARE ANGLICANUM, [TO BE] INTERPRETED. FOL." [*In the Ashmolean
Museum.*]

THIS manuscript was known to and mentioned by Warton and Huddesford, as well
as by Gough, the latter of whom describes it as consisting of corrections and additions
to Adams's *Index Villaris (British Topography*, vol. i. p. 53). It has the following
title-page, but no date : " An Interpretation of Villare Anglicanum. Musæo Ashmo-
leano don^vit Clariss. Author, Jo. Aubrey." The manuscript is evidently the mere
commencement of a work which Aubrey had projected, but was unable to pro-
secute. In a letter to Llhwyd, (dated 1691,) he urges that gentleman to complete
it for publication. In the same letter he says, " Pray register my strawe Tobacco-

box, and M^r Fr. Potter's little Quadrant, and agate-haft." These gifts to the Ashmolean Museum were probably lost or stolen before the year 1824, previous to which date the collection was much neglected.

The above work, of about one hundred and thirty foolscap pages, comprises a list, alphabetically arranged, entitled, " A Collection of British Names of Towns and Rivers out of Villare Anglicanum." Appended is "A Collection of British words that are endenized and now current English, and has escaped the fury of the Saxon conquest" (2 pages); and "Words (now antiquated and obsolete) extracted out of the English Translation of Titus Livius, by Philemon Holland, in 1600. Then in fashion and current English." (4 pages.)

XII. "A COLLECTION OF DIVINE DREAMES FROM PERSONS OF MY ACQUAINTANCE WORTHY OF BELIEFE. 8vo."

XIII. "HYPOTHESIS ETHIC. & SCALA RELIGIONIS. W^th Dr WAPLE, MINISTER OF SEPULCHRES BY NEWGATE."

THESE are not known as separate works; but the first of them probably supplied the materials for the chapter on *Dreams* in Aubrey's printed *Miscellanies*. (See article XXII. in a subsequent page.)

XIV. "A COLLECTION OF GENITURES WELL ATTESTED, 4to." [*In the Ashmolean Museum.*]

THE above collection has never been publicly noticed until the present time. It is a small 4to. manuscript, stitched in parchment, and extends to nearly two hundred pages. It has the title " Collectio Genituarum, Various astrol. mems. Londini, May 29, 1674," and on the outside " 1677. For the Museum." As its name implies, it consists of a series of *genitures, horoscopes,* or *nativities,* embracing those of Aubrey himself, drawn by Coley, which have been already mentioned; others referring to his brother William, to his parents, and to their immediate ancestors. From these have been derived some of the dates embodied in the pedigree of the

Aubrey family (ante, p. 24).   There are also calculations of the nativities of Dr. Dee, Partridge, Hobbes, Dryden, Dr. Charlton, William Penn, Sir William Petty, Sir Christopher Wren, King Charles the Second, and many other celebrated men; also the dates of many principal events in their lives.   The care which Aubrey evidently bestowed upon the collection of these details gives them considerable value as materials for the biographer and literary historian; and the volume is further interesting as it exemplifies the gross absurdities inherent in judicial astrology, in belief of which our antiquary was an infatuated and unfortunate dupe.

XV. " EASTON PIERS DELINEATED."   [*In the Ashmolean Museum.*]

WARTON and Huddesford mention this under its full title, "Designatio de Easton-Piers in Com. Wilts.   Per me (heu!) infortunatum Johannem Aubrey, R.S. Socium.   Anno Dñi 1669."   It comprises nineteen oblong quarto leaves, with " views of the house, gardens, and environs of Easton Piers, drawn in a coarse manner and colouring, but pleasing and expressive."   The view in the title-page of the present volume has been copied from one of these.   A section through the house and garden, north and south, shows that the latter was laid out in the Italian or French mode, upon three different levels, each raised above the other, and ascended by flights of steps, with a "jedeau" [jet-d'eau] in the lowest.   A " grotto, above which, on a pilar, stands a volant Mercury," are delineated in the drawings of the garden.   Six of the sketches represent groups of trees, in different parts of the grounds: others show some of the grottoes in the gardens, and indications of prospects from the house.

XVI. " VILLA, or a DESCRIPTION OF THE PROSPECTS FROM EASTON PIERS."

THIS may have been a companion volume to the above; but it is not to be found.

XVII. "FABER FORTUNÆ, A PRIVATE ESSAY."   [*In the Ashmolean Museum.*]

THE above Manuscript has not hitherto attracted public attention.   It consists of twenty-six small quarto pages, being hints or memoranda of matters desirable for

the public good, or for the writer's personal advantage. The following are extracts:
"1. To get a Patent to open the passage for to make it wider for shippes to come
to Bristowe: whereas now they come no nearer than Hungerode. Also to blow
up the little Island in the key at Bristowe, which occupies the room of two or
three Barks; also to make obtuse the sharp angular rock at St Vincent's, wch
is a great nusance. 2. To put some body upon marying the Thames and
Avon; and to get a share in it." "12. Mrs Hucker advised me to purchase a
barren ground four miles from her estate, wherein is wonderfully rich oare of Anti-
mony and Lead, unknown to the Owner." "18. The institution of my Idea for the
Education of Young Gentlemen in Derbyshire, in Cheshire, London, &c." "28.
Search in the Pety-bag-office, if any Reversions. Gett half a dozen reversions, and
in halfe a year one of them may probably fall. This advice I had from my worthy
friend Mr James Bovey. Get a cole-meter's place. 'Tis worth . . . . . p ann."

Many of the memoranda relate to mineralogical matters; such as alum; calu-
mine; making *latten;* extracting silver from lead; working in copper and brass;
&c. The last entry is a proposition for establishing an office for registering
statistics of various kinds; viz. Births, Marriages, Burials, the Number of Houses,
and Population, Trades, Excise, Church Revenues, Prisoners and Executions,
Shipping, Prices Current, and several other matters which, though little regarded
in Aubrey's time, are now most carefully recorded, and made public.

XVIII. "A COLLECTION OF APPROVED RECEIPTS."——Not to be found.

XIX. "A COLLECTION OF LETTERS, WRITT TO ME FROM ABOUT 100 INGENIOSE
PERSONS: INCH ½ THICK. THIS I DESIGNE FOR THE MUSÆUM." [*In the
Ashmolean Museum.*]

WITH respect to Aubrey's correspondence, it is remarkable that so few of the
original letters of one who maintained a constant intercourse with his literary
friends should be preserved. I am not aware that more than sixty or seventy of
them are to be found, and fifty-six of those are addressed to Anthony à Wood.

After the death of the latter they came into the possession of James Ballard, and form part of his valuable collection of original letters, now in the Bodleian Library, at Oxford. The remainder of Aubrey's autograph letters are scattered through his various manuscripts at Oxford, and there are two short notes in the British Museum. (See *Ayscough's Catalogue*, p. 217.) The letters to Anthony à Wood extend from 1667 to 1694; and, as shown by the frequent extracts in previous pages of this volume, are full of information on the literary topics of the times. They will be found in the fourteenth volume of Ballard's series.

Of equal importance with these is the above-named collection, made by Aubrey, of about four hundred letters written to him, and now preserved, apparently at the instance of Llhwyd, in the Ashmolean Museum. It comprises communications from Sir John Aubrey, from Bathurst, Byrom, Charlton, Sir W. Dugdale, Gibson, Halley, Harrington, Hobbes, Hollar, Sir John Hoskyns, Sir James Long, Llhwyd, Lydall, Sir Isaac Newton, Paschal, Penn, Sir William Petty, Plott, Potter, Ray, Tanner, the Earl of Thanet, Wallis, and many other celebrated men. From some of these we learn that Aubrey took much interest in a popular project of the day, viz. the "Universal Character," or a method of writing to be based upon a due consideration of the philosophy of language. On this subject he corresponded with the Rev. Andrew Paschal, with Seth Ward, Bishop of Salisbury, and Francis Lodwick, one of the attesting witnesses to his Will, ante, p. 60. Many interesting passages might, indeed, be extracted from these volumes, but I forbear quotation, from a fear of making the present memoir too prolix. One of them is a long and very friendly letter from William Penn to Aubrey, dated Philadelphia, 13th June, 1683, in which the writer gives a description of that transatlantic city, and of his government of the little band of colonists under his control. At the end of the second volume are " Letters from D^r Ja: Garden, Professor of Theologie at Aberdene, to Mr J. Aubrey, concerning the Druids' Temples." These comprise only eight of the learned Doctor's epistles; four others were affixed by Aubrey to his *Monumenta Britannica;* and I possess two more : the whole of them are dated between June, 1692, and July, 1695.

Anthony à Wood must have corresponded frequently with Aubrey; but there are only three of his letters in the Ashmolean collection.

Hearne and Warton were acquainted with the volumes here referred to; which have not since attracted the attention they are so well entitled to.

Some letters from Aubrey to Ray were found amongst the papers of the latter, after his death, and published by Derham in his selection of the deceased naturalist's *Philosophical Letters* (8vo. 1718); and a few others, addressed to Aubrey by his friends, have appeared in the anonymous volume mentioned in p. 85, likewise in Warton's *Life of Bathurst*; in the *European Magazine*; in Aubrey's *Surrey*; in his *Miscellanies*; in the *Letters from the Bodleian*; and in Hoare's *Ancient Wiltshire*. Most of these, however, have already been adverted to in the present memoir.

XX. "ADVERSARIA PHYSICA."

BESIDES being mentioned by the author himself, a manuscript with this title is alluded to by Ray (see a letter by him, p. 64, ante). I do not find any such work in the Ashmolean Museum.

XXI. "AN INTRODUCTION TO ARCHITECTURE."

DR. RAWLINSON, in his *Memoir of Aubrey*, speaking of his writings, says, "there yet remains an unfinished piece, *Architectura Sacra*, and as I am told prefixed to one of his MSS. at Oxford." The same statement is repeated in the memoir of 1721 *(Miscellanies)*, with the additional information that the collection "treats of the manner of our Church Building in England for several ages;" and Warton and Huddesford, in their list of the Aubrey manuscripts, mention "Architectonica Sacra: a curious MS., but unfinished."

Aubrey's remarks on architecture seem to have been confined to that of the old churches of England, and, scanty as they are, evince a familiarity with the progressive changes in the forms and decorations of many ecclesiastical edifices in different parts of the Island. Accompanying a notice of the church of Kington St. Michael there are, in the manuscript of his *North Division of Wiltshire*, some sketches of the windows and of the north-doorway,* with notes referring to analogous examples in other buildings. The same sketches and observations were repeated by the author in the first chapter of Part IV. of his *Monumenta Britannica* (to which division of the work he gave the title "Chronologia Architectonica"), and he there extended his remarks to upwards of thirty pages, illustrating them with more than fifty sketches, chiefly of windows and doorways. Some of his remarks are judicious; and there is an approximation to the views now entertained, in his chronological arrangement of the objects he delineates. He says, "The Gothic architecture was a deviation from yᵉ Roman, and yᵉ Gothic Characters a Deviation from yᵉ Roman Characters. Mem. That the fashions of building do last about 100 years, or less; the windows yᵉ most remarqueable: hence one may give a guess about what Time yᵉ Building was."

Passages from this essay may be consulted in Gough's abstract of the *Monumenta Britannica*, in the Bodleian Library; and there is also an imperfect copy of the *Chronologia Architectonica*, in a different hand-writing, amongst Aubrey's papers in the Ashmolean Museum. As already mentioned, some etchings from Aubrey's sketches of windows, &c. were published by Francis Perry in 1762.

XXII. "SOME STRICTURES OF HERMETICK PHILOSOPHY, COLLECTED BY J. AUBREY. Wᵗʰ Dʳ WAPLE."

HERMETIC philosophy has been described as "that which undertakes to deduce all the Phenomena of Nature from three Chemical Principles, Salt, Sulphur, and *Hermes*, or Mercury." (Watt's *Bibliotheca Britannica*.) Aubrey, however, uses the term to denote *astrology*, or matters of mystery and superstition, generally; and describes his *Miscellanies* as "A Collection of Hermetic Philosophy." It is therefore probable that he employed the word with reference to certain writings on astrological subjects, known as early as the third or fourth centuries, and ascribed to an Egyptian sage or deity, called *Hermes* by the Greeks, and surnamed

* The north wall of Kington Church appears to be modern. In the *south* wall there are old jambs, with three-quarter columns to the door-way, indicative of the end of the twelfth century.

by astrologers Trismegistus, or thrice great. These appear to have been really written " at Alexandria, by Gnostic Christians, or philosophers, of the Aristotelian, or of the new Platonic schools." (*Penny Cyclopædia*, article Hermes.) Greek and English versions of some of these writings were published in London, in the seventeenth century, and no doubt contributed to encourage the occult and mystic study of Astrology.

The manuscript which, in 1692, as above-mentioned, was in the possession of Dr. Waple, was doubtless the same which Aubrey afterwards published, with the title of " Miscellanies."

The first edition of the work (1696), and the second (1721), have been already mentioned. A third was "Printed for W. Ottridge, Strand; and E. Easton, at Salisbury," 8vo. 1784*. In the second edition four diagrams, which were engraved on wood for the first edition, occupy a copper-plate at the beginning of the volume, and translations of the Latin passages quoted in the work, are added to the originals. " *Some Memoirs of the Life of John Aubrey*," condensed from the account by Dr. Rawlinson in the *History of Surrey*, precede it; and there is an additional chapter (xxii), entitled, " The discovery of two murders by an apparition." A story from the *Athenian Mercury* is inserted at the end, in compliance with the wish expressed by the author in his letter to Mr. Churchill only a few days before his death (see p. 72, ante). This edition appears to have been printed from a copy corrected by Aubrey. The price of it was four shillings. The third edition has a different title-page, and chapter xii. is there entitled *Miranda* (having previously been headed *Marvels*); but it is in other respects little else than a reprint of the edition of 1721.

The contents of this work, and the opinions of the author, may be inferred from the list of the chapters (ante, p. 2); and that it is frivolous, and replete with absurdities, cannot be denied. In the words of the late estimable Mr. Hamper (*Life of Sir W. Dugdale*, p. 414), it is indeed " a farrago of superstition and credulity." Still it has been the means of preserving some interesting traditionary

* It is stated in Lowndes' *Bibliographer's Manual*, that there were other editions in 1714, 1723, and 1731, but I have not found any authority for the assertion.

R

anecdotes of the times, and affords curious illustrations of the credulity not only of the writer, but of many of his literary contemporaries. The superstitious delusions which were credited when the volume was first printed do not appear to have been wholly eradicated when it was republished, nearly a century later.

Sir Walter Scott derived some aid from Aubrey's lucubrations, in his admirable novel *The Antiquary*, the first volume of which contains several passages clearly suggested by the *Miscellanies*. Indeed the latter work is directly referred to by the novelist; for, in reproving his "sister Grizel" for prolixity, Oldbuck, the antiquary, charges her to "imitate the concise style of old Aubrey, an experienced ghost-seer, who entered his memoranda on these subjects in a terse, business-like manner, *exempli gratia:* 'At Cirencester, 5th March, 1670, was an apparition. Being demanded whether good spirit or bad, made no answer, but instantly disappeared with a curious perfume, and a melodious twang.' Vide his *Miscellanies*, p. eighteen as well as I can remember, and near the middle of the page."

It will be seen on reference to the original that Sir Walter did not hesitate to add to the effect of Aubrey's terse and concise narration by the insertion of a date, "5th March," which is not in the *Miscellanies;* but this is a licence which, in a work of fiction, cannot be of much importance. Sir Walter, indeed, like many other writers of novels and historical romances, often used quotation and authority, more to suit the spirit of his own writings than to honour the author whom he cited. Oldbuck again, terming his sister an "old woman," says, "I include in the same class many a sounding name, from Iamblichus down to Aubrey, who have wasted their time in devising imaginary remedies for non-existent diseases."

A few of the early pages of the *Miscellanies* are expressly stated by the author to be a reprint of some remarks on "Day-Fatality; or observations of days lucky and unlucky," collected by "Mr. John Gibbon (Blew-mantle), and printed in two sheets in folio, 1678." These observations comprise some which bear personal reference to their author, Gibbon; but, overlooking Aubrey's explanation, many of his biographers have regarded them as if written by the latter. Thus it has been said that Aubrey, instead of Gibbon, was born on the 3rd of November, and that he was a considerable loser by the irruption of the sea upon some valuable marsh land in

Kent, part of an estate which had been left to him; but a more careful examination of this Essay proves that the passages in question do not relate to Aubrey. In like manner some pompous Latin verses by Gibbon, celebrating the birthday of the Duke of York (afterwards James II.) have been attributed to Aubrey.*

The anonymous letters printed in the *Miscellanies* on the subjects of " Transportation in the Air by an Invisible Power," and " Second-Sighted Men in Scotland," were written by his friend and correspondent Dr. Garden, of Aberdeen.

Besides the manuscript literary works by Aubrey, preserved in the Ashmolean Museum, there is a small packet, marked (apparently by Malone) " Loose Papers (I believe) in Mr Aubrey's hand." Amongst these is the *Draught of his Will*, prepared between 1652 and 1659, which has been given in page 33, and a sketch of a *dramatic piece* which Aubrey contemplated writing. It seems to have been intended for a comedy in five acts, but the first three scenes alone are written, and those in a very rough and confused manner. The heads of the succeeding scenes are indicated; and a careful examination of the manuscript might develope the author's intention. The play was to be called " The Country Revell,† or The Revell of Aldford," and the following are some of the " Dramatis Personæ:" . . . . . Courtoise, a Knight of the Bath, and Protector and Servant of distressed Ladies; Lady Euphrasia, wife to Sir Libidinous Gourmand; Lady Florimel, wife to Sir Surly Chagrin; Justice Wagstaff (Sir J. Dunstable); Sir Fastidious Overween; Captain Exceptious Quarrelsome; Country Wenches and Fellows; Ballard-singer, &c. On the title-page is written, " Scene, Aldford in Cheshire, by ye River Dee.

---

* It will be seen that the statement as to Aubrey's marriage, already refuted, is not the only error in previous notices of Aubrey. He is often said to have been at school with Hobbes at Leigh-de-la-Mere, which has been shown to be incorrect; and his memorable interview with Charles the Second is stated to have occurred at Stonehenge instead of at Avebury.

† A revel or wake is an annual rustic festival, generally limited to country villages, or hamlets, not sufficiently populous to support a fair. Shakspere uses the word *revel* to denote a feast of riotous and noisy jollity.

St. Peter's Day 1669." "Act I. Scene 1.," however, is " Christian-Malford Green. Enter Country Wenches." Christian-Malford is a parish in the immediate vicinity of Aubrey's birth-place.

In October, 1697, four months after Aubrey's death, some remarks by him on " a medicated spring at Lancarim, Glamorganshire," were published in the *Philosophical Transactions* (No. 233, p. 727).

THE preceding narrative, with the extracts and comments on the life and writings of Aubrey, may be considered by some readers as too minute; perhaps even as frivolous and unworthy of publication; but I am well satisfied that there are many others who will wish they had been extended, especially when it is known that the materials for doing so were not deficient. Aware of the impossibility of pleasing all, I have been influenced by the expressed wishes and opinions of those antiquaries whose judgments I respect; and in what is here put on record, I have endeavoured to develope the personal and mental characteristics of the man, as well as the spirit of the age in which he lived and acted; and these will be found to reflect each other vividly and tangibly. Had Aubrey associated with men of high intellect; had he lived in the present times of political, literary, and scientific high-pressure power, he must have greatly distinguished himself, for he evidently possessed that element of sympathy for art and nature which is the germ of greatness. The appalling and degrading fanaticism, with the frivolous superstition which pervaded society, in town and country, in college and at court, could not fail to influence and corrupt the general character of all persons who came within their respective influences. Even Milton and Dryden, his contemporaries, and Johnson in a later and more enlightened age, were not exempt from certain notions of bigotry and superstition. Few are the persons, and rare their occurrence, who can stand so far aloof from their associates, as to think and act with perfect freedom, independent of contemporary prejudices and conventionalities.

FINIS.

INDEX.

s

LONDON:
J. B. NICHOLS AND SON, PRINTERS, 25, PARLIAMENT STREET.